| DATE | | | |
|---|---|---|---|
| DEC   4 1980 | MAR 6      1985 | APR 2 0 1993 | |
| OCT 1 4 1982 | APR 2 8 1986 | | |
| NOV 4 - 1982 | NOV 2 6 1986 | | |
| FEB 1 0 1983 | NOV 3 0 1987 | | |
| MAR 5 1 | OCT 23 '88 | | |
| OCT 5   1983 | DEC 15 '88 | | |
| OCT 1 9 1984 | SEP 1 9 1991 | | |
| OCT 2 6 1984 | OCT 1 6 1991 | | |
| NOV 1 5 1984 | FEB 1 3 1992 | | |

# DEADLY BUGS AND KILLER INSECTS

## OTHER BOOKS BY HAL HELLMAN

Navigation—Land, Sea and Sky
The Art and Science of Color
Controlled Guidance Systems
Light and Electricity in the Atmosphere
The Right Size: Size, Form and Function in the Animal
    World
High Energy Physics
Defense Mechanisms, from Virus to Man
The City in the World of the Future
Helicopters and Other Vtol's
Energy and Inertia
Biology in the World of the Future
The Lever and the Pulley
The Kinds of Mankind: An Introduction to Race and Racism
    (with Morton Klass)
Feeding the World of the Future
Population
Energy in the World of the Future
Transportation in the World of the Future
Communications in the World of the Future
Technophobia: Getting Out of the Technology Trap
Understanding Physics (with Ludwik Kowalski)

# DEADLY BUGS AND KILLER INSECTS

## HAL HELLMAN

## M. EVANS and Company, Inc.
New York, New York 10017

*Library of Congress Cataloging in Publication Data*

Hellman, Harold, 1927-
  Deadly bugs and killer insects.

  Bibliography: p.
  Includes index.
  SUMMARY: Describes a variety of bugs and insects and their harmful effects on the health of man and his pets and livestock.
  1. Arthropoda, Poisonous—Juvenile literature.
  2. Insects, Injurious and beneficial—Juvenile literature.
  3. Dangerous animals—Juvenile literature.
  [1. Arthropoda, Poisonous.   2. Insects, Injurious and beneficial.   3. Dangerous animals]   I. Title.
  QL434.45.H44      595′.2′0469      78-17403
  ISBN  0-087131-269-7

M. Evans and Company, Inc.
216 East 49 Street
New York, New York 10017

Design by Robert Bull

Manufactured in the United States of America

9 8 7 6 5 4 3 2 1

79 - 319

# Contents

**1** SMALL & DANGEROUS 9

**2** TOOLS OF THE TRADE 23

**3** STINGERS, SCRATCHERS, & SQUIRTERS 45

**4** BITERS, BURROWERS & BLOODSUCKERS 75

**5** DISEASE CARRIERS 111

**6** INSECTS VS. MAN 141

SUGGESTED READINGS 171

INDEX 179

PICTURE CREDITS 189

The author wishes to express his thanks to the many persons who kindly provided material and information for this book, including Prof. O. R. Taylor of the University of Utah; Lt. Col. A. A. Hubert and Lt. Roy M. Garrigues, III of the Armed Forces Pest Control Board; J. D. Atwell of Phoenix, Arizona; Prof. J. H. Humphrey of the Royal Postgraduate Medical School in London; Prof. A. W. Benton of the Pennsylvania State University; Dr. Samuel G. Breeland of the Bureau of Tropical Diseases (HEW); several anonymous correspondents at the National Center for Health Statistics and Dorothy M. Staats at the U.S. Department of Agriculture; and to Mrs. Josephine Jurasich, for a fine typing job.

But mainly he wishes to express his deep appreciation to Dr. Roger Williams, Professor of Public Health (Medical Entomology), College of Physicians and Surgeons at Columbia University. Prof. Williams not only provided extended technical review, giving generously of his valuable time in the process, but supplied interesting material and illustrations as well.

# 1 SMALL & DANGEROUS

"Lodgings—free from bugs and fleas,
   if possible,
If you know any such."

Aristophanes (446–380 B.C.)

Mr. Jomo gazed proudly at his new house, and thought about his plan. He was going to rent out the house rather than live in it, and use the income to enjoy some of the luxuries of life.

The house was located on a nice street just outside the city limits of Nairobi, the largest city in East Africa. That would surely make it easy to get a tenant. All in all, things were looking very good; the project was, he felt, worth all the time, effort, and expense that had gone into it.

But Mr. Jomo's pleasure didn't last long. Before he could find a tenant, an ominous buzzing sound began to be heard inside one of the walls. Bees! A swarm of wild African honeybees had somehow found its way into one of the walls and decided to make its home there.

Now, we are often told that bees and hornets will not sting unless molested; if we leave them alone they will return the favor. And in truth the bees in the wall of Mr. Jomo's house were content as long as left alone.

The problem, of course, was that no one would rent the house as long as that sound was heard, which meant that Mr. Jomo was the unhappy owner of a very expensive hive. This went on for two whole years. Finally a friend of his contacted an American specialist in bees, who happened to be teaching at the University of Nairobi, and asked for help.

The specialist, Dr. William F. Lyon, and an assistant went down to the house to look the situation over. First they put on their protective bee veils, gloves, hats, and overalls. They made sure that the onlookers—perhaps a hundred people, along with many chickens, goats, and pigs——were moved at least 40 to 50 yards away from the house. Then the assistant (without Dr. Lyon's approval) pried open part of the board siding on the house.

"That," says Dr. Lyon, "was the mistake!! Bees came boiling out of their nest literally by the thousands, swarming and stinging everything in sight. The entire sky seemed to become darkened by the rapidly flying honeybees. ... The women, children, and livestock were rapidly reached. Most everyone seemed to be crying and screaming, covering their bodies with blankets, while the goats, cattle, pigs, and chickens were helpless. The bees entered the huts by the hundreds, stinging old persons, who were unaware of what was happening. . . . Soon, the bees managed to get under my veil and stung me in the ears, nose, cheeks, eyelids, forehead, etc. I found myself chewing bees in my mouth and spitting them out. . . ." *

Dr. Lyon and his assistant beat a hasty retreat, of course, then returned later and did some spraying with an insecticide.

By the time the "smoke" had cleared, several children were in the hospital and quite sick, while Dr. Lyon could hardly walk or talk. His legs were so badly

---

* "My Experience With the African Honeybee," *Gleanings in Bee Culture*, November, 1974, p. 335.

swollen they looked like small tree trunks. Fortunately his wife had brought along some honeybee serum when they came to Kenya, and taking some of this prevented the results from being even worse than they were. Fortunately, too, no one in the village died. Two goats and one chicken were killed by the stings, however, and a number of animals were seriously injured.

But there was a happy outcome. The bees were gotten rid of and, as a bonus, the villagers were treated with two huge washtubs full of beautiful honey, which they considered a great treat.

This story, which is quite true (though Mr. Jomo is not the homeowner's real name), tells us two things about the African honeybee—it is a great producer of honey, and it is far more aggressive than the kind with which we are familiar.

**AGGRESSIVE BEES**   While the bees in our story were a "wild bunch," the domesticated African bees—kept as in many parts of the world for their honey and wax—have the same traits. In 1956 some of these African bees were imported by a Brazilian beekeeper with the idea of crossbreeding them with the local Brazilian species. His objective was to combine their greater productivity with the more peaceful ways of the local type.

It was an interesting idea, but it didn't work. And the worst of it all was that the far more aggressive African bees escaped. There was still the possibility that they would interbreed naturally with the local wild bees, of which there were of course far more; but often, instead of interbreeding, they simply took over wherever they landed. In such cases they would raid an existing nest, kill the queen, and install one of their own. In short order a peaceful colony became a vicious, mean-tempered one.

Nor are the African bees the only aggressive ones in the world. A Briton, J. W. Beagle-Atkins, once reported a personal experience with the tree bees of northeastern India. These may be even more evil-tempered than the African ones. For no apparent reason a swarm of thousands may rocket down in a mass attack on an unsuspecting passerby. After one such attack, during which Mr. Beagle-Atkins was stung some 2,000 times, it took more than six months before he had fully recovered.

The ancient Greeks and Phoenicians are reported to have used these insects as a very effective weapon; they would catapult closed vessels of bees onto the decks of enemy ships, unloosing a swarm of very angry bees. There are not many sailors who would remain at their posts while being attacked by a cloud of angry, stinging bees.

As a result of the introduction of the African bee into Brazil, the number of fatalities there from bee stings has increased considerably. Though figures in many areas of the country are hard to come by, one expert, Dr. X. Hubbell, estimates that there are now 400 deaths a year from bee stings in Brazil. The African bees have, as a result, been nicknamed the "killer bees." They have also been expanding their territory and are estimated to be moving north at the rate of some 200 to 300 miles a year. This means they will reach the United States, unless something unforeseen happens, in 13 to 19 years, the latter figure being the more likely one.

Professor Orley R. Taylor, who has been studying the African bees, says that though they are a tropical species, they have the potential to tolerate conditions in the southern half of this country. With reference to the potential danger he says, "It *seems likely* that we could cope with the aggressive bees if they arrive in this country." (Author's emphasis.) When read carefully, this is seen to be an optimistic statement, but one with ominous undertones.

Dr. Taylor feels, however, that the fearsomeness of killer bees is somewhat exaggerated. He says, for example, that he has been stung by both South American ("Africanized") and domestic (U.S.) bees and that he cannot tell the difference in severity. He also feels, in contrast with some other experts, that as the killer bees move northward, they will interbreed with local species. Time will tell. (For a frightening picture of

The Brazilian ("Africanized") honeybee

what could happen if a species of overgrown, vicious bees really got out of control, read Arthur Herzog's chilling novel, *The Swarm*.)

But bees are by no means the only insect killers. At least 50 people die each year in the United States as a direct result of bites and stings of venomous animals and insects.* It is estimated that more than half of these deaths are caused by insects and their cousins, the spiders, scorpions, and other such creatures. Death from bee sting is more common than from snakebite, however. While this seems surprising at first, we shall see later that there is a good reason for it. The situation in Central and South America is even worse; in Mexico alone, there are 70,000 cases of scorpion sting yearly, and 1,200 deaths.

**Major groups covered in this book**

*Phylum*                               **ARTHROPODA**

*Class*                  INSECTA   ARACHNIDA
MYRIAPODA

*Order*                  HEMIPTERA

---

\* There are undoubtedly other deaths that are not recognized as such and are attributed to other causes.

**BUGS AND INSECTS**  The words *bug* and *insect* are both used in two ways. To a person who studies these creatures (called an entomologist) the words have very specific meanings. A bug is an insect, for example, but an insect is not necessarily a bug. That is to say, bugs are a subdivision (order Hemiptera) of the wider class called Insecta. Examples are bedbugs, shield bugs, and assassin bugs.

Spiders and scorpions are in a class all their own; they are called arachnids (class Arachnida) and have, for instance, eight legs rather than six as do the insects. Centipedes, on the other hand, are in a group called the Myriapoda (many legs).

As shown in the chart, however, there is a grouping that includes all of these, and that is the phylum Arthropoda (Ar throp′ o da). Members of this very large group are characterized by:

**a)** An exoskeleton, i.e., a nonexpandable, outer, protective covering, generally of a hardened, horny material, which must be shed in order for the arthropod to increase in size.

**b)** Externally jointed appendages or limbs (i.e., "arms" and legs), which permit the creature to move, manipulate objects, and feed; they often act as external sensors, and are sometimes used to inject poison into another animal.

And in insects:

**c)** A body composed of more or less similar segments arranged one behind the other; collections of segments are grouped into body regions such as head, thorax, or abdomen. These regions are not always observable, however.

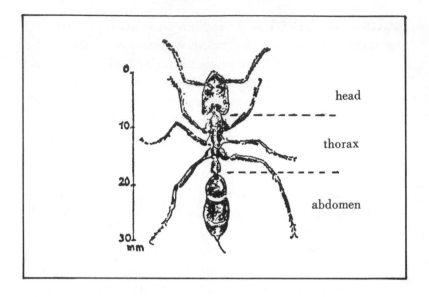

Segments of insects are collected into three body regions (head, thorax, and abdomen) as in this giant of the ant world, the Argentine *Dinoponera*. Note that the six legs are attached to the thorax region. The pair of appendages on the head are antennae.

The arthropods are a highly successful group, containing perhaps a million different species. The complications of classifying them tax taxonomists to the extreme. Fortunately we needn't be concerned with these complications. For in this book we are going to use the *un*scientific meaning of the words *bug* and *insect,* namely any creature that is small but not microscopic, and dangerous to the health of man and is pets and livestock. While this group involves only a small percentage of all arthropods, even one-tenth of 1 percent of a million species is still a lot of bugs. Many insects also attack man's crops. While this is an important group economically, it is beyond our sphere of interest.

The balance of the million species either have little to do with people or are actually beneficial. The praying mantis, as well as wasps and ants, prey upon many of the venomous creatures we will be discussing. Insects also act as a food source for desirable fish and birds. And bees do far more good than harm; about one-third of our total diet is directly dependent on bee-pollinated plants. (In many plants, the transfer of a substance called pollen is absolutely necessary before seeds can develop.)

In arachnids, there are either one or two body regions. The soft tick (which averages between .5 and .75 cm. in length) is an arachnid, not an insect, and has four pair of legs.

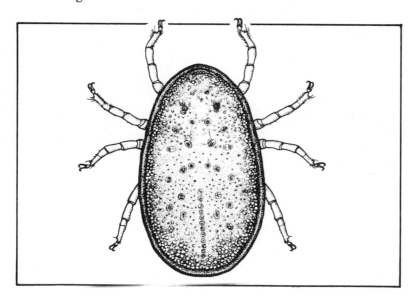

Of the unknown millions of arthropod bites and stings in the United States each year, there are some 25,000 severe reactions and, as we have already noted, about 50 deaths. (In a large-scale study made between 1950 and 1959, H. M. Parrish found that arthropods accounted for 65 percent of the 460 reported deaths caused by all venomous animals in the United States. His findings are interesting and are summarized in the table.)

| VENOMOUS ANIMAL GROUP | | HUMAN DEATHS (1950–1959) |
|---|---|---|
| Hymenoptera | | 229 out of 460 or 49.8% |
|   Bees | 124 | |
|   Wasps | 69 | |
|   Yellow Jackets | 22 | |
|   Hornets | 10 | |
|   Ants | 4 | |
| | 229 | |
| Snakes | | 138 out of 460 or 30.0% |
| Spiders | | 65 out of 460 or 14.1% |
| Scorpions | | 8 out of 460 or 1.7% |
| Others | | 20 out of 460 or 4.4% |

Clearly if you are bitten or stung ("envenomed"), the likelihood of severe reaction or death is small, unless you are the victim of certain arthropods. Part of our aim in this book is to enable you to recognize these particular creatures. The best approach, of course, is not to get envenomized at all. Surprisingly, there are steps you can take to insure this. We will learn about them, too, as well as what you can do if you get bitten or stung by a venomous arthropod.

But bugs are not troublesome to humans only because of their bites and stings; even more troublesome from a medical point of view is the fact that they are vectors of disease, meaning that in some way or other they cause sickness in man or animal. A century or so ago, no one seemed to know this. Today we know that they are responsible for the spread of several hundred different diseases! The World Health Organization has reported that of all the human deaths, human illness, and human deformities on the face of the earth, fully half can be attributed to arthropods and to the diseases they transmit!

"Throughout history," writes entomologist L. H. Newman, "many a military campaign has failed because the armies were stricken with disease spread by insects. Whole civilizations have declined because the vigor of their peoples was undermined by malaria and other illnesses. Vast regions of the world have long remained undeveloped and almost uninhabited because insects made it imposible for men to settle in them."

So now you know where we are heading—into the world of deadly bugs and killer insects, in all their gory glory. Let us start our expedition with a look at some of the means by which these creatures do their deadly work.

# 2 TOOLS OF THE TRADE

"... great ugly things, all legs and wings,
With nasty long tails arm'd with nasty long stings."

Rev. R. H. Barham (1799–1845)

A favorite theme of monster movies is the man-sized insect. Happily we need not worry about such creations in real life; insects can assume their many weird aspects because they are small and much less affected by gravity than we are. Thus an East Indian horsefly, *Pangonia longirostris*, can have a proboscis ("nose") three or four times the length of its body, and a tropical bee, *Euglossa cordata*, can have a tongue that is longer than the rest of its body. But on the scale of human life, such monstrously long appendages would be pulled right to the ground by gravity. In other words, these "monsters" can exist in miniature or in great size via trick photography, but not in great size in real life.

This is not to say, however, that insects and bugs do not have some incredibly powerful tools with which to carry out their activities. Insects tend to be specialized, and most are noted for some specific activity. Chewing insects, for example, may have extremely powerful jaws. Termites are well known for what they can do to wood. In their blind search for food, however, they can damage many materials they do not normally eat. As they tunnel through the ground, they may eat right through plastic-covered and even lead-covered electrical cable, shorting out electrical systems. Some insects can cut through concrete and mortar, and even through hard metals such as silver and copper.

Artillery shells have been found to be damaged by a large species of beetle.

More commonly, insect mouth parts are adapted for piercing and sucking so that they can feed on the blood of animals, or perhaps on the sap of plants. In the latter case, pressure from within the plant is usually enough to move the sap into the insect. With blood-suckers, however, there is likely to be a strong pumping mechanism which the insect uses to draw in the blood.

Sometimes, as with the spider, the piercing mouth parts are used to inject a poison into its prey, usually an insect—either to paralyze it or to liquify the victim's

The head of a female black widow spider, greatly enlarged

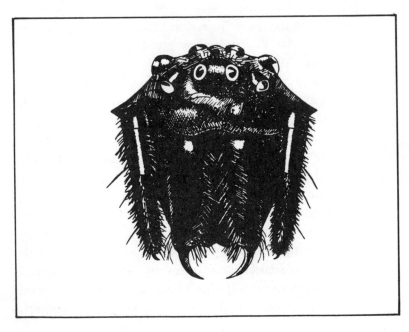

insides, which can then be drunk like a malted milk.

In other cases, the piercing apparatus is in the tail, and is used for laying eggs. These, if laid in a living thing, may later create their own damage when they begin to feed on the victim's tissues. Or the piercing instrument may be specifically intended for defense.

**BITING AND STINGING**   At this point it might be well to distinguish more carefully between biting and stinging, which are often confused with each other. Biting insects make use of some aspect of their mouth parts, no matter whether these parts are specifically adapted for chewing or piercing and sucking. (It sometimes helps us think more kindly of the insect world if we keep in mind that in either case they are merely trying to get their food with these instruments; their purpose in life is not to make us miserable, although they often do.) Horseflies and stableflies have sharp mouth parts which can inflict painful bites. The long proboscis of the Indian horsefly *P. longirostris*, mentioned at the beginning of this chapter, can inflict a painful bite right through thick clothing.

Indeed, the name *mosquito* has a common origin with the word *musket;* it derives from the Latin word for fly, *musca,* and has to do with the musketlike projection (proboscis) on the insect's head.

In stinging insects, on the other hand, the abdomen or rear section of the female ends with a dagger, syringe, or saw. In these insects, as we have seen, the instrument in question has to do with egg-laying, which is why it is the female that is so equipped. Insects in this group include bees, wasps, ants, and sawflies.

Generally, bees and wasps will only sting when squeezed or otherwise annoyed. They will attack and sting an intruder that enters or approaches the nest, for example.

The wasp stinger is smooth and the insect can easily remove it from the victim after use. As shown in the drawing, the honey bee stinger is a more complicated device consisting of two barbed pieces that work separately. After the initial puncture, one holds its place while the second is worked further into the skin; then the roles are reversed.

The barbed sting of a honeybee

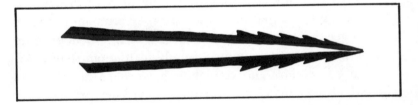

In some cases the actual physical damage inflicted by the insect may in itself be a problem. The stable or dog fly is a vicious biter and may account for serious blood loss in domestic animals. And the chigoe flea, once it penetrates the skin, may actually burrow into the skin tissue. But in general, insects are so small in comparison with humans and even most pets and livestock that the physical damage they cause (other than annoyance and some pain from the biting, stinging, or piercing operation) is of less interest to us than the other means they have at their disposal for doing their work, namely venoms, poisons, and toxins.

**VENOMS, POISONS, AND TOXINS**  Though these three terms are often used interchangeably, they do have fairly specific meanings. A toxin is a substance of complex chemical nature produced by living organisms such as bacteria, plants, and animals, which causes sickness in other living organisms. There are also relatively simple chemical substances produced by plants which are also poisonous, such as vegetable alkaloids,* but we are not concerned with these. Nor are we concerned with other substances that may be highly toxic to humans and pets but are of nonbiological origin and simple chemical nature. Such substances are properly called poisons.

Toxins are produced by bacteria, plants, and animals. We, of course, are most interested in the final group, those produced by animals. The technical name for these is zootoxin, or more commonly, venom. Thus the scorpion is more properly called a venomous than a poisonous creature.

The venom of some creatures, e.g., the scorpion, comes in two basic varieties. One of these produces only a local effect, meaning the reaction is restricted to the area of the sting. The result might be a sharp pain with swelling and numbness, all of which usually disappear in a few hours or so. The result, then, is equivalent to a hornet or wasp sting. Most European and American species of scorpion produce this kind of venom.

The second type is a so-called neurotoxic venom

---

* Poisonous alkaloids may also be made by living organisms, such as the puffer fish.

(affecting the nerves), which results in symptoms similar to those of strychnine poisoning—the victim may experience immediate sharp pain, followed by a wide range of symptoms, including general numbness and drowsiness; speech impairment and tightness of jaw muscles; muscle twitching, spasms, and paralysis; nausea; breathing difficulty; impairment of the blood circulation system; and, if untreated, possible death. This neurotoxic venom is produced by *Buthus occitanus* in Europe, and by several common species in the Americas, including *Centruroides suffusus* in Mexico and *C. sculpturatus* and *C. gertschi* in the southwestern United States. We shall learn more about these arachnids in a later chapter.

Venoms are made in special body cells. In some venomous creatures, such as certain frogs and toads, the cells are on or near the skin surface. These cells just break down and release their moist, toxic secretions on the surface of the skin. In other cases, as in the clusters of venom-producing cells around the spines of venomous fishes, sharp-edged spines are smeared with venom when the thin covering membrane is damaged.

In insects (and snakes) the cells are clustered together to form glands and the venom is stored in small sacs. When the insect bites or stings, venom is squeezed out of the sac into the wound, or it is injected through a hollow fang or sting.

Venom glands have an interesting similarity to our own digestive glands. When we eat, our digestive glands produce a complex assortment of enzymes which act to rapidly break down the tissues in the food we have taken in. Venom glands also produce such en-

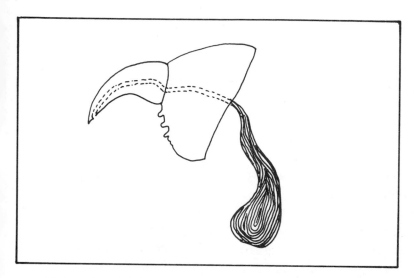

Poison gland and fang of a spider

zymes but contain in addition the poisonous substances
that do their other damage.

In general, venoms must be injected into the body
in order to act. They will not, as will many poisons and
toxins, cause trouble if taken by mouth. Thus when one
is bitten by a venomous snake (or spider or scorpion)
it is considered relatively safe to suck out the poison by
mouth through an incision made directly over the fang
marks. Naturally, if another kind of suction is available,
it should be used.

Further, this method should only be used if the
venomous animal is known to be a dangerous one, and
if the victim is more than two or three hours from medical help. This is particularly true if the bite is on a fin-
ger or toe, or the back of the hand or instep of the foot,
where there are arteries and tendons near the surface.

Cutting one of these can spell much trouble. But if real danger threatens then the "cut and suction" method should be used. It will reduce the amount of toxin in the victim's system and could result in saving his or her life, even if not all the poison is removed.

**POTENCY OF VENOM** What we are concerned with here, in other words, is the amount of venom involved, as well as its potency (strength). The venom of the black widow spider, for example, has been found to be several times more potent than that of the cobra, and 15 times more powerful than that of a rattlesnake. Does this mean that a bite from this spider is therefore several times more dangerous? Not at all, for the cobra will deliver much more venom in its strike. A large cobra is said to be able to deliver up to 13 cubic centimeters (about 13 grams!) in a single bite.

| SPIDER | INTO THE BLOOD STREAM (mg) | UNDER THE SKIN (mg) |
| --- | --- | --- |
| *Latrodectus m. mactans* (black widow) | 0.110 | 0.200 |
| *Lycosa erythrognatha* (wolf spider) | 0.080 | 1.250 |
| *Phoneutria nigriventer* (tropical tarantula) | 0.006 | 0.0134 |
| *Trechona venosa* (funnel web spider) | 0.030 | 0.070 |

As a result of the foregoing comparisons, though, black widow venom has gotten the reputation of being one of the most potent of all animal venoms. But experiments were performed on the lethal effects of various spiders, i.e., determining how much of each venom was needed to kill mice. The results, shown in the table, were surprising.

It can be seen that the last two spiders have venoms that, against mice anyhow, are several times more potent than that of the black widow. The potency of these venoms is matched by that of the more dangerous scorpions, the sea wasp jellyfish, two sea snakes, and two species of frogs! The latter two, however, produce contact poisons, and as we shall see later, these are less of a threat than those that enter our systems. The last three spiders in our table are restricted to Central and South America.

As a point of information, the average yield of venom from a black widow spider is 0.060 milligram (dry weight), while that of the tropical tarantula is twice as high. Clearly, part of the seriousness of a reaction will have to do with how much venom is injected into one's system. Even the bite of a black widow spider is not always fatal. We shall have more to say about this later.

You may have noticed that in pointing out the potency of the *P. nigriventer* and *T. venosa* venoms, we specified that they were several times more potent than the black widow—"against mice anyhow." The point is that we cannot be certain that this is the case in humans, for different animals may have different responses to a given venom.

For example, the dose of rattlesnake venom needed to kill the common southwestern woodrat is 140 times that needed to do in a mouse. This has to do with the woodrat's blood chemistry. The Mexican ground squirrel, a vicious little creature that can kill a rattlesnake, also seems to be practically immune to the venom. Researchers are trying to find out what it is that confers this immunity; perhaps it can be put to use to provide protection for humans as well. Another important point, which we have already hinted at, is the size and condition of the victim. Thus a child or a sick person may die from a bite or sting that would only sicken a healthy adult for a short time.

**ALLERGIC REACTIONS** Bees, wasps, hornets, yellow jackets, and ants are all part of a larger group called Hymenoptera. While we will describe them in more detail later, there is something very special about all their venoms that requires some discussion here.

In general, the sting of a hymenopteron is not as dangerous as that of, say, the *Centruroides* scorpion. The normal response is pain, itching, or swelling at the site. This is called a local effect. It may take multiple stings, 30 or more, to produce what we call a systemic reaction, meaning a generalized effect on the body. Under such a mass attack, the venom attacks the red blood cells and the nervous system to produce hemorrhages, anemia, and nerve paralysis. In severe cases, say 200 stings or more, death is likely if immediate treatment is not obtained. But the reaction of some persons to a hymenopteron sting is a different matter altogether. These people are so sensitive to certain materials in the venom that it is dangerous for them to receive even a single sting. They are said to be hypersensitive, or allergic, to the venom.

When an allergic person is stung by any of these insects, he or she may go into anaphylactic shock (fall

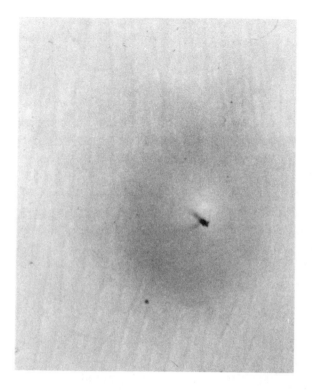

American honeybee sting showing resulting swelling

unconscious) in a few minutes, with death a possibility. Other symptoms include uneven heartbeat and pulse, faintness, flushing of the skin followed by paling, collapse of blood circulation, abdominal cramps, and diarrhea. These may precede or follow such common allergic symptoms as swelling, skin rash, and wheezing.

Under certain circumstances, a single hymenopteron sting may be dangerous even to a nonallergic person, i.e., where the person's normal supply of adrenalin has been depleted. This can occur in heat stress, for example. A case was reported a few years ago of a teen-aged boy in New Jersey who died from a bee sting. He had been stung on other occasions and had never had any systemic reaction at all. But this time he was mowing a steeply sloped lawn in hot weather and, it is believed, his state of exertion made the difference. Tests on mice seem to bear out the conclusion that a sting may be more dangerous when the body's adrenalin is low.

The *Military Entomology Operational Handbook* points out: "While truly 'unprovoked' stinging of large animals is considered quite rare, very little provocation is needed to incite some wasps and ants to attack intruders in the areas of their nests. Whatever their reasons for stinging, the Hymenoptera kill more people in the United States each year than do snakes and spiders combined."

It is also believed that a large number of additional deaths result from such stings but are blamed on other causes because they are undetected as sting reactions.

As a result the American Society of Allergists devotes a fair-sized portion of its yearly meeting to medical aspects of insect allergy, and to the Hymenoptera in particular. An important area of basic study is simply trying to understand why some persons are sensitive and not others. One theory suggests that sensitivity is built up somehow, as opposed to being genetically "built-in," as in typical allergies. About one person in every hundred is allergic to insect sting. How can a person tell if he or she has this problem? Usually the diagnosis comes when a reaction is serious enough to require medical aid. But susceptibility can be suspected if an individual shows progressively stronger local reactions to stings.

There is a way of lessening the sensitivity of such people to hymenopteron sting, using a series of shots. Naturally, the doctor doesn't want to cause a serious reaction, so the initial injection may contain only a millionth part of the venom in a single live sting. (It is possible to determine by tests whether a person is allergic to just one or two of the insects; in such case the treatment would involve the venom of only the offending type of insect.)

In the following visits, the amount is increased steadily to a given point, which is thought to be strong enough to create immunity. For strongly allergic persons, this size dose may continue to be given every couple of months for several years, or in extreme cases, for an indefinite period. A year's treatment requires venom from 20 to 30 insects.

How does one find out if the treatment is working? The only sure approach is to "challenge" the patient with an actual sting from the type of insect in question. Imagine how you would feel in such a situation—the thing you fear most in this world provides the only way you can be tested. But, of course, the sting is being given under tightly controlled conditions, with the doctor standing by and ready with immediate treatment if necessary. This is surely far better than being accidentally stung when you are out camping or hiking, or even in the back yard. In some cases, every minute counts.

Until fairly recently, the accepted desensitizing method was to use injections of whole body extract (WBE), made by crushing the bodies of the major stingers—bees, yellow jackets, wasps, and hornets.

Some researchers now believe, however, that the job can be done much better with pure venom than with WBE. But obtaining the venom presents something of a problem, for it is not yet available commercially. Federal regulations controlling the movement of new drugs to the market are strict. And pure venom is certainly a drug. It must be proved that the substance both works and is safe for humans to use. But it is the large drug companies that are best able to do this testing; and they are reluctant to spend the time and money needed to test and bring such a substance on the market, since the market is relatively small. Whole body extract has been on the market for years.

Collecting pure venom is, at the moment, more of an adventure than a business. At Penn State, where research is going on in this area, it has elements of a military expedition. Armed with garbage can, carbon dioxide fire extinguisher, and ladder, the collector goes forth. Scaling the ladder and clinging to roof or eave, the collector squirts the insect nest with $CO_2$ from the fire extinguisher. This cools and puts the wasps or hornets out of commission long enough for him to knock the nest into the garbage can and clap the lid onto it.

Back at the laboratory the insects, nest and all, are put into a freezer; when they are immobile their venom sacs and stingers are removed.

Obtaining honeybee venom is easier. It has been found that when an electric grid is placed under a hive, a low voltage shock causes the bees to sting a special membrane which automatically collects the venom. The membrane is then removed from the nest and the

## TOOLS OF THE TRADE

Two ways of obtaining pure venom. Above, an electrified box is placed near a nest. The disturbed white-faced hornets sting a layer of filter paper. Though less venom is collected this way, it is pure. Below, a white-faced hornet, fresh from the freezer, has its venom sac removed. The sac is then punctured, releasing the venom.

venom taken from it. As shown in the photo, this method can also be used for hornets and wasps.

Proponents of the pure venom treatment feel that when whole body extract is obtained, enzymes (chemicals) in the insects' bodies may well destroy some of the venom. Defenders of the WBE treatment maintain that one or more allergens (the active parts of the venom) may be present in the insects' bodies as well as in the venom, and that desensitization using WBE therefore makes sense. The situation, as you can see, is still unsettled, though the champions of the pure venom approach seem to be gaining momentum. Another problem is that immunization against one type of insect does not necessarily work for the others.

For allergic persons who have not gone through the desensitizing process, or for whom it has not worked, special kits are marketed, as for example the Insect Sting Kit of Nelco Laboratories. These contain, among other things, a substance called epinephrine (adrenaline), which acts to relieve the symptoms and prevent the more serious consequences. The kits contain all the equipment necessary for injecting the substance, and sensitive individuals are advised to have one available whenever there is a chance of being stung.

There is also a service called Medic Alert, in which persons with any medical problem or condition that cannot be easily seen or recognized wear a bracelet or necklace pointing out the problem, such as "Allergic to Insect Stings." Thus someone who appears on the scene might be alerted to the problem if the victim is no longer able to speak. A central telephone number is also given in case any special instructions, which are kept on file, must be obtained.

A powerful description of what life can be like for someone who is allergic to one of these insects (and for whom whole body extract did *not* work), is given in "The Sting of Death," an article in the August, 1976, issue of *Good Housekeeping*. It was written by George B. Brownell, whose special problem was the yellow jacket. His love of the outdoors caused him to have several narrow scrapes with death.

For a while, things were so bad that he wore a complete beekeeper outfit, including white overalls, gloves, and headgear equipped with a mesh veil, whenever he went outdoors, even into his back yard. But one day he neglected to use it and was stung by a yellow jacket. He tells us in the article that the medical report on his condition stated simply, "Complete vascular collapse due to hymenoptera sting." (Vascular collapse means that his body was unable to supply blood to vital organs, especially the brain.) Though he managed to give himself a shot of adrenaline, he thought it was too late. He writes:

> But I needed no medical report to diagnose my own reaction. It was something far different from my previous experiences. Just before giving myself the shot, I felt myself slipping away. Completely away. I was going out like a candle. And, I thought: "This is what it is like to die." I was finally and fully aware that—despite *anything* I could do—a tiny insect could actually extinguish my life.

You will be happy to know that Mr. Brownell got medical aid in time and did not die, and that a new series of shots, with pure venom, subsequently cured him of his allergy.

But immediate allergic reactions are not the only ones to be feared. Dr. Robert E. Arnold reports in *Field & Stream:*

> At the opposite extreme from these quick allergic explosions are delayed symptoms that lay low for as long as two weeks before attacking the victim's health. It has been known for years that wasp stings can cause severe bleeding and damage to the kidneys and blood vessels, but now doctors are finding that *Vespidae* (wasp) stings damage the brain, spinal cord, and nerves with alarming frequency.

In general, however, the sooner a reaction comes, the worse it is.

**FANTASTIC VARIATION**  Arthropods show remarkable variation even within the constraints of small size. An interesting aspect of the phenomenon is how many different ways have developed among them for envenomizing their victims. Spiders use fangs, rather like a snake's; centipedes use what is the equivalent of their first pair of legs; the mosquito injects its venom (an irritant, really, the main point of which is to keep the victim's blood from congealing before the meal is finished) with its long, pointed proboscis; bees, wasps, and hornets, as we have seen, use a stinger at the base of the tail. The scorpion, one of the most dangerous of all the creatures we will study, also uses a stinger at the point of its tail but can bring this tail over its head and sting its victim in this way. Some ants have a sting

# TOOLS OF THE TRADE

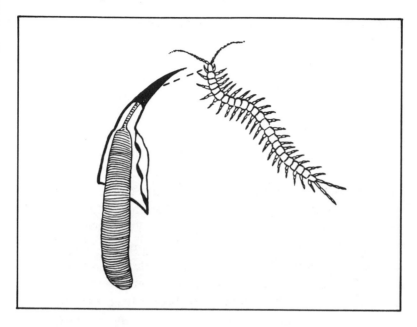

Venomous fangs of the centipede are modified legs of the first body segment

like the bee's, but in others the sting has been replaced by a squirting apparatus through which its venom can be discharged, and a third group can both bite and sting.

In yet another approach, the caterpillars, cocoons, and even adults of some species of moths are covered with hairs or spines that cause severe inflammation when they come in contact with one's skin. The venom may come from an opening at the tip of the hair or a part of the hair may break off in the wound and release the venom. These are called nettling or urticating hairs.

Some insects may be venomous at one stage of

their lives but not at another. The adult yellow flea beetle is relatively harmless, but the Bushmen of the Kalahari Desert in Africa use the pupae and larvae of the beetle (stages of development between the egg and the adult) to make a poison for their arrows.

A final variation is seen in insects that are not venomous but are repellent in some way. They may secrete some unpleasant substance on the surface of their skin, or may spray it when attacked, as in the case of the well-known stink bug. Or the insect may simply have something in its own system that makes it taste terrible when taken in by a bird or other predator.

Another aspect of the great variability in the insect world is size. For while human-sized insects are an impossibility,* there are some that come very close to being monsters. The rhinoceros beetle from Central America, *Megasoma elephas,* is about five inches long. Perhaps the largest living insect is *Erebus agrippina,* a moth from Brazil with a wing spread of eleven inches. There is also a fly from South America, you will be happy to hear, that grows up to 11.5 centimeters (4.5 in.) long.

Happily, as with snakes, the larger creatures are less likely to be the venomous ones. Indeed (though this is most likely a coincidence), the killer bee is slightly smaller than its European cousins. But as we shall see, even the tiniest arthropods can do plenty of damage.

---

* For a discussion of why this is so, see *The Right Size* by H. Hellman, Putnam, 1968.

# 3 STINGERS, SCRATCHERS, & SQUIRTERS

"The ant has made himself illustrious
Through constant industry industrious.
So what?
Would you be calm and placid
If you were full of formic acid?"

Ogden Nash

Among American Indians in the older days, stories told around the fire held the same important place that comic books, novels, or perhaps television hold today. Particularly intriguing was the so-called trickster cycle, sometimes considered the most distinctive form of Indian story. In it, a character is made to suffer because of some defect in his character or some specific bad thing he has done. The following example comes from the Jicarilla Apache Indians of the American Southwest.

Yellow Jacket is walking along one day carrying a bag and meets Coyote, who asks what he has in the bag. Yellow Jacket answers that it contains his children, but Coyote doesn't believe this and keeps bothering Yellow Jacket to tell him what is in the bag. Yellow Jacket finally "admits" that there is fruit in the bag. Coyote slyly offers to carry the bag for Yellow Jacket, but as soon as it is handed over, Coyote runs home. He calls his family to come and have some fruit.

He puts his hand in the bag and promptly gets stung. Thinking he must have stuck his hand on a thorn, he puts his hand in again and is stung several times. In yanking his hand out he breaks the bag and discovers to his horror that Yellow Jacket had indeed been telling the truth. Yellow Jacket's children fly out and attack Coyote's whole family. Coyote ends up with his face so swollen he cannot even open his eyes. (Note

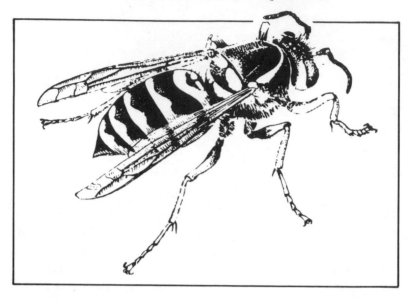

Yellow jacket

that Yellow Jacket is the "good guy" in this tale.)

Yellow jackets, hornets, *Polistes,* mud daubers, and the cicada killer are all wasps, a highly varied group of insects that kill many harmful insects found around homes and gardens. But they may attack people as well as insects.

Wasps tend to be elongated, with three distinct body regions (head, thorax, and abdomen) and four wings. While all can sting, *Polistes,* and especially yellow jackets and bald-faced hornets, are considered the most dangerous because of their aggressive behavior, their abundance, and their likelihood to be found near humans and to sting if a person comes near their nests. They may even nest in the walls of homes.

Although it takes an expert to classify wasps by

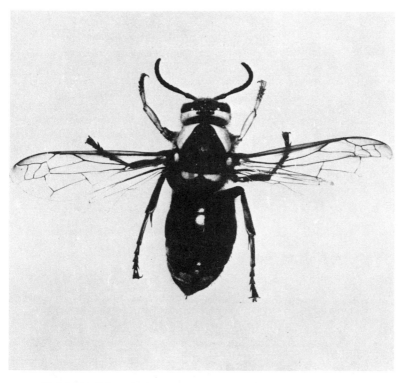

Bald-faced hornet

appearance, yellow jackets and bald-faced hornets are easily identified from the paperlike nests they build; yellow jackets build nests of varying size, some underground, some hidden in rock, in home walls, or under logs. Hornets and *Polistes* nest in the open—in trees and shrubbery and under the eaves of houses. The nests of hornets and yellow jackets are football-shaped and are covered with an envelope of a paperlike substance, while those of *Polistes* are open and resemble a honeycomb.

White-faced hornet nest

Polistes nest

The mud daubers are also easily recognized from their mud nests, which are usually built in the corners of man-made structures.

These are all social wasps, meaning that they nest in groups. The reason they are particularly dangerous is that blundering onto their nests can result in attack by many wasps, each of which can sting several times. There are also many types of solitary wasps—rugged individualists—but these tend to be both less aggressive and less abundant.

The female velvet ant (mutillid wasp)

There is an important exception to this rule (that the social wasps are the most dangerous), and that is the female velvet ant. Though it is wingless and looks very much like an ant with a colorful, hairy rear end, it is actually a wasp. An adult velvet ant (technically mutillid wasp) may grow to 2.5 centimeters (an inch) long, and like other wasps the female has a powerful stinger which can inflict an extremely painful sting with potentially dangerous aftereffects. Though found mostly in the southern and western parts of the United States, one species is common on the sandy beaches of Lake Erie and can make life very unpleasant for barefoot bathers. In some regions these mutillids are referred to as cow killers and mule killers. Though this is almost surely exaggeration, the sting is certainly lethal to insects such as the bumblebee, the nest of which the velvet ant parasitizes.

We keep using the word *dangerous* in discussing these insects. But danger is a relative thing. Today, due to insecticides, flies can be pretty well controlled in houses and other closed areas. In earlier days this was not so, and it was not too unusual for a householder to use a hornets' nest inside the house to help get rid of houseflies. The bald-faced hornet, especially, catches many houseflies as food for its young. In other words, it was felt that the relatively small chance that a member of the household would get stung was more than counterbalanced by the fly-free atmosphere. (There was little chance of blundering into the nest, which was placed high up.)

An excellent example of how a stronger arthropod can turn hunter into hunted is seen in the wasp/spider relationship. The spider, as we shall see, is a potent predator, catching many kinds of insects, large and small, in its web, injecting a paralyzing poison, and eating them.

Although predator wasps are often smaller than the spiders they go after (such as the tarantula and the bird spider of the tropics, which has a three-and-one-half inch body!), they are tough, powerful attackers who paralyze their prey with a well-aimed sting in a nerve. This puts the spider's legs and jaw pincers out of action, after which the wasp buries it. The large, juicy body of the spider thus remains alive and fresh and provides nourishment for the offspring of the wasp.

**BEES** Wasps, hornets, bees, and true ants (which we'll get to later in the chapter) are, as we know, members of a larger group called Hymenoptera. This is an order containing many species of diverse form and habits. One factor they all have in common is that the rear section (abdomen) is connected to the middle one (thorax) by a slender waist. Indeed, the words *insect* and *entomology* (the study of insects) both mean "cut in."

As with wasps, there are many families of bees, but only two, honeybees and bumblebees, are considered dangerous. Bumblebees are large and furry and are colored black and yellow or black and reddish. In flight they make a loud buzzing noise. Their nests are generally on or in the ground, often in abandoned field-mouse or chipmunk nests. Though two or three times larger than honeybees, they are neither as aggressive nor as abundant and so are considered less dangerous. Like wasps, the bumblebee can withdraw its stinger after stinging and use it again.

Bumblebee

The honeybee is about the same size as a yellow jacket (roughly 1.3 cm. or .5 in. long) and is also striped. But the yellow jacket's stripes are a clear, bright yellow with black between, while the honeybee's stripes are mixed with an amber-colored fuzz, perhaps from contact with pollen. Both bees and wasps tend to have hairy midsections, but on close examination, the wasp's hairs will be seen to be smooth while the bees' are feathery (for retention of pollen). Honeybees will also be seen to have pollen "baskets" on their hind legs, in keeping with their way of life. Another difference is that bees feed pollen and nectar to their young, while wasps feed insects and spiders to theirs.

But when you are pestered by a yellow and black insect at a picnic, it is most likely to be a yellow jacket. Honey- and bumblebees are more likely to mind their own business if you mind yours. If alarmed, however, they can release "alarm odors" called pheromones which cause other bees nearby to attack. The honeybee, it should be noted, loses its stinger in the attack and dies as a result; it is the only hymenopteron of which this is true.

At the height of its development a honeybee colony may have 50,000 individuals or even more. Part of their life cycle involves swarming, or a full-scale migration to new quarters. If ever you should find yourself near a swarm of bees it would be best to stay perfectly still. If you begin to run, you may attract them, and they can generally fly faster than you can run. If you

Honeybee

should find them coming right at you, the best thing to do is just lie flat on the ground. Wild honeybees tend to nest in trees, and if you are standing, they just might mistake you for a tree! Even if some should land on you, it would be best to lie still, if you can. But if they should start to sting, then is the time to get up and run like blazes.

If you are stung by a honeybee and are allergic to its venom, or even if you're not, the sting should be pulled or scratched out with the fingernails as quickly as possible, for muscles in the sting will continue to pump venom for several minutes. It is important not to pinch or push the stinger further into the skin as this may cause further venom to be injected.

**BEEKEEPING**   With all this, many hobbyists keep honey-bees, including at least one enthusiast in an apartment in Manhattan! But in many suburban areas, complaints from neighbors who are becoming more aware of potential danger are forcing some of the hobbyists to give up the hives they keep, or at least to cut down on their number.

On the other hand, higher sugar prices and the increasing interest in natural foods have caused an increase in the number of hives. In my state, New Jersey, about 4,000 beekeepers maintain about 45,000 hives. (The total number of beekeepers in the United States is apparently unknown. Current estimates run between 200,000 and 300,000.)

New Jersey has no state law regarding beekeeping, though regular inspections are made of the hives that do exist. Different localities have different rules, however. The Board of Health in the town of Tenafly recently forced a beekeeper to move his hives out of the community, whereas a Municipal Court judge in Garfield worked out a compromise in a case that only cut down the number of hives a hobbyist was permitted to keep. In Brazil, however, beekeeping as a hobby has just about disappeared!

It is interesting to note that honeybees are not native to North America, though there are a number of species of native wild bees. All the present honeybees originated in Europe, Africa, and Asia, having been carried over to the New World by colonists who brought beehives with them. The first record of honeybees in North America dates back to 1638. The first record of honeybees anywhere dates way back to the Stone Age, as for example in a cave painting at the Arana (spider) Cave in Spain.

The harsh winter of 1977, plus problems caused by pesticides, has started rumors of a honeybee shortage. Allergic persons and others afraid of insects might call that good news, but honey lovers, as well as farmers who depend on bee pollination, certainly would not. It is worth noting that professional beekeepers often rent hives to fruit orchards and truck farms for this purpose. California farmers alone contract with beekeepers for almost a million colonies to pollinate crops worth $500,000,000. The bees work right alongside the farm laborers. But the bees are cultivated, not wild, and tend to be of a rather placid nature. Their hives are clearly marked so that no one blunders into them. Wild bees, not to speak of the Africanized ones, are much more unpredictable and would hardly be welcome company for the farm hands.

While we have seen that there are treatments for

hymenoptera stings, the best approach, of course, is to try not to let it happen in the first place. The table shows a list of suggestions that will decrease the likelihood of your getting stung.

But if you do get stung, and if you are allergic to bee venom, here is some small comfort. Recall that the treatment for a hypersensitive person who has been stung is a shot of adrenalin. Our own body systems, however, are built to inject adrenaline into our blood streams when we are under stress—which includes fright! Thus the more panicky you are, the better your chances may be for survival!

## HOW TO DECREASE THE LIKELIHOOD OF BEING STUNG

1) *Avoid flowers, flowering trees,* and shrubs where bees are gathering honey.
2) *Avoid exposed food.* Take care in the storing and disposal of food, particularly in warm weather. Keep it in closed containers. Spray garbage cans with insecticides.
3) *Avoid strong perfumes, particularly floral fragrances,* in cosmetics, hair sprays, tonics and suntan lotions. Bees are attracted to odors.
4) *Avoid bright clothes.* Wear no flowered prints or rough cloth. Black seems to attract insects. The recommended colors are white, green, tan, and khaki.
5) *Avoid excessive exposure of skin area.* Wear shoes at all times; also wear long pants, long sleeves, socks and hats.
6) *Avoid nests.* Insects sting when they are touched. Avoid the areas of their nests. Nests are best de-

stroyed at night when insects are inactive.

7) *Avoid quick or sudden movements.* Do not run or flail arms as this seems to excite insects to sting.

8) *Avoid driving with windows open.* Wind may carry an insect in and cause driver to be stung. Gently guide insect to open window with folded map or newspaper.

9) *Avoid open doors and windows.* Use adequate screens on home windows and doors.

10) *Be aware that bees become angry and sting more frequently on bright warm days,* particularly following a rainfall which has washed the nectar from the flowers.\*

(Nelco Laboratories, Inc.)

**ANTS**  Ants can be distinguished from other, similar insects by their long, thin "waists" between thorax and abdomen (like some wasps), and especially by their elbowed or bent antennae. They are among the most numerous of all animals on earth, both individually and in numbers of species. Probably as a result of the large number of species, this insect has developed a remarkable number of forms of defense and offense. Most female ants, in keeping with the fact that they are Hymenoptera, have stingers. Some, like the Argentine ant widely found in warm parts of the United States and the large black carpenter ants found throughout the country, bite but do not sting. Some, like the acrobat ant, and the huge *Myrmecia gulosa* (2 cm. or .8 in.

---

\* It is also believed that bees sting more readily just before a thunder storm, perhaps due to a rapid change in air pressure, or some electrical effect.

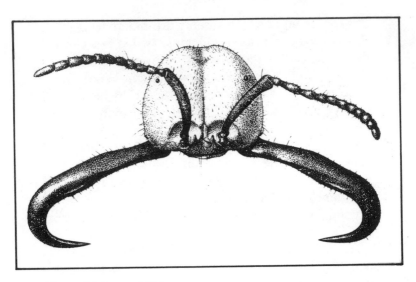

Powerful jaws of Eciton

long) in Australia, both bite and sting. *Formicinae,* found in temperate climates, have no sting but can spray a notable quantity of poison containing almost 50 percent formic acid. In some cases, the ant will bite and then spray the acid into the wound. The famous driver or army ants of Africa and South America are basically stingers but swarm in such huge numbers that practically nothing living can stand in the way of one of their advancing armies. Anything caught in the march is stripped clean to the bone by their powerful jaws in short order.

In the United States the worst aggressors are the fire ant and the harvester ant, both fierce stingers. As a matter of fact, the fire ant has actually done what the Africanized bee may or may not be in the process of doing in South America, namely, wiping out another

Fire ant

species. The fire ant was accidentally imported into Alabama from South America along with some plants early in this century. Since then, as shown on the map, it has spread rapidly throughout the South.

Depending on the species, fire ants vary in size from small to large (1.6 mm. to 5.8 mm. or $\frac{1}{16}$ in. to $\frac{1}{4}$ in.). They may be brownish red; or they may be multicolored, with the head and part of the thorax yellow, dark red on the rest of the thorax, and a brown to black abdomen. But they are most easily recognized from their nests, which are raised earthen mounds some 30 to 90 centimeters (1 to 3 ft.) high, leaving the surrounding vegetation practically untouched. More than 157 million acres in the United States are infested with the ant, often 50 mounds to the acre and with one report of 130. These mounds interfere with ploughing and harvesting; the ants can damage a number of crops

STINGERS, SCRATCHERS, & SQUIRTERS

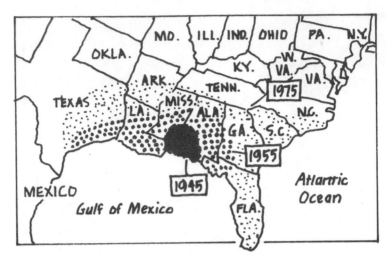

Spread of the fire ant

A fire ant mound is hard enough to damage farm equipment.

directly, including citrus trees, soybean plants (a very important crop), seed potatoes, and others; they attack the offspring of poultry and livestock; and they attack humans as well. So vicious is their sting that farm workers who have been stung by these creatures often refuse to go back into the fields.

The immediate reaction to such a sting is a fierce burning pain lasting some minutes, followed by formation of raised wheals on the skin and fluid-filled sores, with associated pain and tenderness. After three to eight days the sores will heal but may leave scars. Allergic persons may also experience systemic reactions—wheezing, cramps, vomiting, dizziness, confusion, shock. Death is rare but has been reported. The American Medical Association declared the fire ant a health hazard at its 1971 annual meeting.* Local first aid involves washing sting sites with soap and water, applying ice packs or cold compresses, and applying a paste of baking soda and water.

Harvester ants, though two to three times larger than the most troublesome of the fire ants, are somewhat less of a problem. Though their sting is also vicious, they have not spread the way the fire ant has. They are red to dark brown but, like the fire ant, are

---

* In the July, 1976, issue of *Audubon Magazine*, however, Anthony Wolff maintains that the fire ant menace has been exaggerated—that they rarely damage crops, and that they are not nearly so ferocious as has been claimed, particularly in a report in *Newsweek* (April 26, 1976). He admits, however, that, "there is still enough evidence of the ant's medical importance to sustain a lively controversy. . . ." Further research is being carried out.

most easily recognized from their living quarters; these are not so much raised mounds as large, clear smooth areas that may be up to 9 meters—30 feet!—in diameter. Harvester ants are very active and aggressive in protecting their nests. Found mostly in the warm, dry areas of the Southwest, they destroy vegetation and tunnel so extensively that paved roads and airstrips will sometimes be undermined and collapse.

There are a number of other stinging and biting ants in the United States, but unless one happens to be allergic to their venom, they are much less of a problem than the fire and harvester types. Ant venoms seem in general to be somewhat similar to that of the bee. *Myrmicea* venom, for instance, contains histamine.

Those that spray the formic acid bring up an interesting problem, however. The substance is obviously contained in their systems; indeed the red ant was at one time the sole industrial source of formic acid. Yet the material is poisonous to other insects, and to the red ants themselves! Now, it is known that our own stomachs secrete hydrochloric acid to help digest our food, and that this acid is injurious to the stomach wall if the two come in contact. The secret, it was finally discovered, is that the stomach also secretes a kind of mucous which protects the walls when the acid is present. Some similar mechanism may protect the ant when it injects or sprays the acid, but this is not known for sure. The importance of these substances to the ants is seen in the fact that the poison sac of *Formicinae* (which has no sting, remember) occupies a full fifth of the abdominal cavity, and it is full of formic acid at high concentration. The ant specialist Remy Chauvin writes:

STINGERS, SCRATCHERS, & SQUIRTERS

I cannot resist quoting some startling figures here: in the course of a fight a worker may discharge 1 mg. of poison, which is equal to 0.5 mg. of formic acid. Suppose you try the experiment my assistant and I carried out in the Vosges mountains [in northeastern France]. We mercilessly stirred up an enormous nest, bigger than both of us; like us, you would have to retreat half asphyxiated [choked] by formic acid. If we suppose that the nest had only 50,000 ants spraying us, which is nothing, that is equal to 25 g. [almost an ounce] of formic acid. Much less would be enough to stop the respiration of several men.

Fromica ant spraying its venom

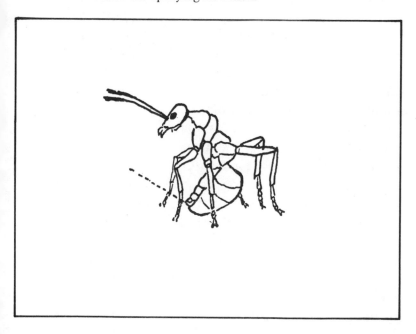

Though we are speaking of ants here, it should be pointed out that other insects also spray their poison. One species of assassin bug can squirt a venom up to a foot with great accuracy. Its effect on human skin can be quite severe, and it can cause temporary blindness if received in the eye. The bombardier beetle can accurately fire its venomous spray a distance of 20 centimeters. The bumblebee also is said to be able to squirt its venom.

Returning to our ants, we know that some, such as the wood ant *Formica rufa,* may, instead of spraying its poison, bite with its sharp jaws and then squirt the powerful acid into the wound.

Ants, like bees and wasps, are social insects. Thus a nest contains not only strong, healthy adults, but defenseless eggs and young in all stages, plus a queen who must be protected at all costs. Flight under attack or annoyance makes no sense biologically. The only sensible thing to do is attack. Looked at in this way, the response of the ant colony to Prof. Chauvin's actions was perfectly reasonable.

But there are differences among species. Some of the more timid species will turn tail and head back for the nest if attacked outside. Others, like the red ants of the woods, *Formica,* are more aggressive; they will stay and try to fight off the attacker even from outside the nest. Thus, Prof. Chauvin adds:

"We had to turn tail for, in a few seconds, the ants covered us with an angry army, half stifling us with their spray of formic acid." (There have been some reports of hymenoptera chasing their victims, sometimes for a considerable distance. One researcher was chased more than half a mile by a hive of Africanized bees!)

Ants have been around a long time, and, not surprisingly, some of the early peoples looked upon them with awe. The Mayas, for example, attributed eclipses to the periodically aroused appetite of ants, which then ate away part of the celestial bodies. But the early peoples also apparently put the ants to work for them. Native Indians in South America tell stories of punishment given to criminals involving ants. Victims were bound to tree trunks in areas of army ant invasions. Within a short time they were reduced to skeletons.

**SCORPIONS** Another arthropod, whose sting is even more deadly, is the scorpion. It is more deadly in the sense that its sting can be dangerous to anyone, not just to persons allergic to its venom. The reason there are many more deaths from hymenoptera stings is that the total number of bee stings is far, far higher. For this we can thank the scorpion's secretive ways; scorpions hunt at night, seizing insects and spiders with their large claws. If the prey resists, the scorpion swings its tail over its head and thrusts in a poison-bearing, needle-sharp stinger.

In other words, the scorpion, like most arthropods, is a shy creature and will only sting a human if caught in clothing, stepped on, or whatever. The results, however, can be severe, as we noted in Chapter 2. In spite of the fact that they sting, not bite, they are arachnids, not hymenoptera. Thus they are related to the spiders. The sting in scorpions has nothing to do with egg-laying, as in bees and wasps. In fact, the scorpion gives birth to live young. These ride around on the mother's back for about a week, and then are on their own.

Though scorpions range in size from 2.5 to 20 centimeters in length (1–8 in.), it is not necessarily the larger ones that are the most dangerous. In the United States the two most dangerous are members of the *Centruroides* group. Both are found mainly in southern Arizona and parts of nearby states. They are straw yellow, and one of the species has two irregular black stripes on its back. Their length ranges from about 5 to 8 centimeters (2–3 in.).

The *Androctonus* scorpion is responsible for many deaths yearly in the Middle East and North Africa. It has a bulb of venom and a stinger at the tail end of its body, and a strong pair of pincers at the other end. It grasps its prey with the pincers and, when necessary, whips its tail over its head to use its stinger.

Local first aid for scorpion stings should include ice packs and application of a tourniquet if possible close to the sting site but between the sting and the body. There are, fortunately, antivenins available for the most dangerous species.

An indication of the general feeling about scorpions is seen in some of the early names given to it:

Palamneus—murderer
Miaephonus—stained with blood
Vaejovis—god of the underworld
Pandinus—quite terrible.

**CONTACT!**   There is another group of arthropods that are venomous in a slightly different way; they release toxin on contact with the victim. These, as we noted in Chapter 2, fall into two general groups, both with fancy names. The vesicating arthropods are those that release some sort of fluid from portions of their bodies just from contact with the skin of another organism. The blister beetle, found mostly in the western United States, is one of the best known. Even the light pressure exerted when a person brushes against one of these is enough to cause release of the fluid, which contains cantharidin. This is a powerful substance that has long been used for certain medical purposes to cause blistering. While the result of contact is a relatively mild, though sometimes extensive, blistering, it is worth noting that human skin is quite a tough material, and the fact that there is any response at all from mere surface contact is a tribute to the chemical strength of the toxin.

Blister beetles are long and narrow, with a "neck,"

Blister beetle

and range in length from 1 to 2 centimeters (.4–.8 in.); they vary in coloration and are attracted to bright white light, so many cases occur at night near such lights. They are also plant feeders, with the result that persons moving through bushes containing such beetles end up with mysterious blisters and wonder where they came from. If you find one of these creatures on your skin blow it off, don't slap at it, as you might a fly or mosquito, for slapping will cause a maximum dose of the vesicating agent to land on your skin.

The second group of arthropods we are going to

Puss moth caterpillar

discuss also release their venom on contact, but through the agent of tiny hairs or spines. These break off upon contact and lodge in the skin of the victim; thus the result can be, and often is, much more severe. Caterpillars tend to be the worst offenders here; these are called urticating or nettling caterpillars (from a family of plant nettles with stinging hairs called *Urtica*).

Caterpillars, as you probably know, are the larvae of moths and butterflies. The puss moth caterpillar, for example, is a cute, furry little creature, but underneath that fur coat there are many short hollow spines connected with poison glands. These break on contact with the victim's skin, permitting venom to enter and resulting in an immediate sharp pain. This is followed by reddening, swelling, and numbness, which may be ac-

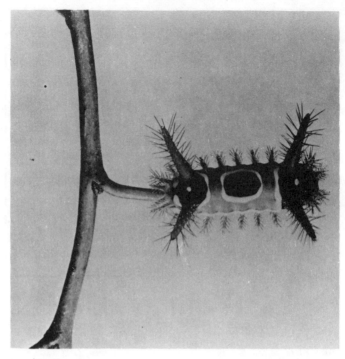

Saddleback caterpillar

companied by nausea and vomiting. These creatures, found mostly in the Southeast, vary from 2 to 3 centimeters (.8–1.2 in.) in length, and are tawny (tan) to gray in color and light to dark in shade.

Another troublemaker is the saddleback caterpillar, so-called because its coloration gives the appearance of a dark saddle on a greenish blanket. Close examination of this two to three centimeter long caterpillar reveals clusters of spines all around its body. The effects of its venom can be very severe and can cause extreme pain. As in all cases of urtication, the effects will vary widely, depending on how much venom has entered one's body.

Perhaps best known, however, is the Io moth caterpillar, widely found in the eastern and central states. It is about 5 to 8 centimeters long, which means it is larger than the puss and saddleback types, and it is a handsome animal, with strips of red or maroon and white along its pale green body. Many of the spines clustered around its body are venomous, with their tips connected to large individual poison glands.

Other urticating caterpillars are those of the white-marked Tussock, the flannel moth, and the brown-tail moth. The spines of this caterpillar break off easily and may be carried by the wind. On striking exposed skin they may cause intense itching. A similar result may obtain if the hairs lodge in clothing hanging out to dry; they can cause severe skin trouble when the clothing is eventually put on.

Though these urticating caterpillars generally come out only at particular times of the year, it is a good idea to be wary of handling or touching any furry caterpillars. Problems arise mostly, however, when the victim accidentally comes in contact with infested vegetation. Clearly long pants and long sleeves are a good idea when in such an area.

Local first aid calls for removing the spines as soon as possible ( by repetitive application and removal of cellophane or adhesive tape); ice packs; and application of a baking soda/water paste. For severe pain various kinds of medical treatment are available. It is interesting to note that aspirin seems not to be effective.

Aside from the problem of pain, when should you

seek medical help? The question you should ask is whether you are experiencing an effect that is not local or restricted to the affected site. Dr. Robert E. Reisman, former Chairman of the Insect Committee at the American Academy of Allergy, says it is a good idea to seek medical help for any kind of serious reaction, such as fainting, swelling or blocking of the throat, falling blood pressure, wheezing, coughing, or shortness of breath.

# 4 BITERS, BURROWERS, & BLOODSUCKERS

a man thinks
he amounts to a lot
but to a mosquito
a man is
merely
something to eat

Don Marquis, in *the life and times of archy and mehitabel*

Not long ago a young child, normally frisky and healthy, became tired and sickly. He had no temperature but there was an even more alarming symptom: he began to lose feeling and control of his limbs.

No one could figure out what was wrong. Test after test was tried, with no success whatever. The boy began to slip into unconsciousness.

One day a nurse who happened by his hospital bed had a hunch. She ran her fingers through his hair and found what she suspected—a small tick had found its way into his scalp, had clamped its jaws into the skin, and had begun to suck the boy's blood, at the same time injecting a poison into his system.

But, you may wonder, how can the tick go through this whole process without the victim's feeling anything at all. The answer is that the tick moves very slowly and stealthily—it has a very gentle touch. In addition, many ticks also release a mild anesthetic when they feed, which masks the piercing process.

Ticks are not insects but wingless, flattened, leathery arachnids. Note in the illustration that they do not have the cut-in shape typical of insects, that the two rear sections, thorax and abdomen, are joined. Ticks are common in wooded areas and will often take up a position at the tip of a leaf, with forelegs outstretched. A tick may remain in this position for days or even

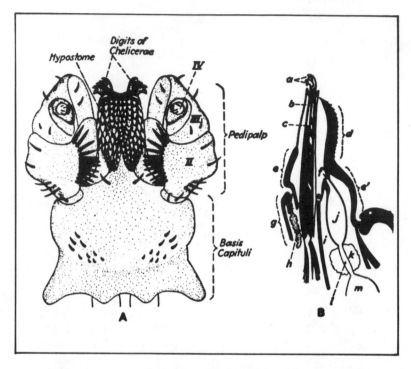

Anchoring type of mouthparts found in ticks. Diagram
at left (A) is a bottom view, clearly showing how anchoring teeth are slanted backward for better gripping, and
cutting organs ("chelicerae," pronounced ke liss er ee).
(B) shows a sectioned side view; the part marked *c* is
the so called rod of the chelicera, which slides in and
out of the sheath *b* when used. It is interesting that the
brain of this creature *k* is right next to the stomach *m*.

weeks, waiting for an animal to pass within touching
distance, in which case its claws catch onto the fur—
or the clothing of a person. Then it will crawl slowly,
slowly about until it finds a suitable place. If the victim
feels something at this point, the tick is easily brushed

off. After it digs in, however, it is much more difficult to dislodge, for its head actually becomes buried in the skin.

Once this happens, a human victim can make it remove itself by applying lighter fluid or alcohol, or bringing a source of heat such as the tip of a burning cigarette to it (not at the same time as the fluid is used, of course). Sometimes it can be scraped off carefully with a knife, or pulled out with a firm yank by tweezers. But if pulled out carelessly or in panic, its mouth parts may remain embedded in the flesh and a local infection can result. Do not use an insecticide on it; some will surely get into your wound.

Due to ticks' habits they often have to go for long periods without food, but once they find a suitable host, their capacity is astonishing. Most ticks are smaller than five millimeters (about .2 in.) long; as they have their dinner, however, they may expand to the size of a marble.

The bite of the tick may cause anything from severe pain and other local reaction, to paralysis, to death. The Center for Disease Control reports a steady increase in Rocky Mountain spotted fever,* carried only by ticks, since about 1960, probably due to the increasing activity in hiking and camping. There were a total of 906 cases in 1976, and 1,100 (and 70 deaths) in 1977. Symptoms include fever, chills, head or muscle aches, and swollen tissues. A rash appears on the wrists and ankles after a day or so.

---

* Now frequently called tick-borne typhus.

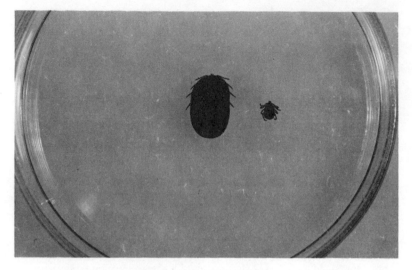

Ixodid ticks, engorged and unengorged

Although the disease may occur anywhere in the United States, including 27 cases on Long Island in 1977, four states—North Carolina, Virginia, Tennessee, and Oklahoma—account for more than half the reported cases. In general, however, ticks are most common in the Southwest, where the cost of injury to cattle alone is in the millions of dollars.

Dogs and doghouses can become heavily infested with the brown dog tick. This may lead to discomfort to the dog as well as weight loss and unsightly appearance. The dogs may then bring the ticks into homes, where they can be a serious nuisance. Around the turn of this century, ticks were reported so numerous in some European villages that the inhabitants were forced to leave. Today, ticks can be controlled with pesticides, but it is worth noting that the brown dog

BITERS, BURROWERS, & BLOODSUCKERS

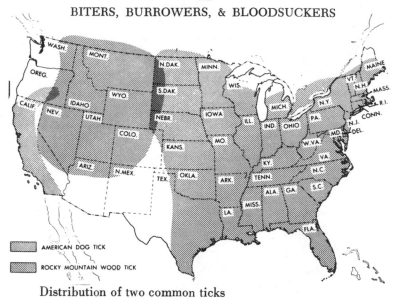

AMERICAN DOG TICK

ROCKY MOUNTAIN WOOD TICK

Distribution of two common ticks

tick has developed resistance to certain of the pesticides that were at one time effective.

In the wild, most small fur-bearing animals are
host to large numbers of blood-sucking ticks. The new-
born of even larger species, such as deer, may well
bleed to death if too heavily infested with those pests.
(Could this be one reason why humans evolved without fur?)

**PARASITES** Ticks are parasites, which means they attach
themselves to an animal, called the host, and then live
at least a part of their lives on the host. Parasites may
or may not harm the host; but by definition they are
dependent on it and may also lay their eggs on it.

Ticks are external parasites. Even more common
are internal parasites; these are usually worms of some
form, such as the fluke, tapeworm, and trichina, which

Life history of Rocky Mountain wood tick and American
dog tick

inhabit the digestive or blood system. And of course
microorganisms are also parasites. Many of these parasites cause anything from discomfort to death. We'll
have more to say about insect-caused disease in the next
chapter.

Among other parasitic insects that attack animals
and humans are mites, lice, certain flies, and fleas.
These, at some stage of their development, are perma-
nent parasites. Others, such as horseflies and mos-

quitoes, feed upon their hosts for only short periods, thus spreading out their attentions.

There are also hyperparasites, which means parasites of parasites. For example, one type of wasp (the ichneumon) may lay its eggs in a caterpillar, upon which the hatched larvae feed. Thus it is a parasite. But the larvae in turn may then be parasitized by a smaller wasp, such as a chalcid.

**MITES**  Mites are smaller, sometimes microscopic, versions of ticks, the skin of which is not leathery. Mites may

Photo taken through microscope shows chigger mite *T. akamushi* with mouthparts (two dark probes) embedded in a section of rat skin, and an actual tube in the skin formed by the digestive juices of the mite, through which it draws in its food—dissolved tissue cells.

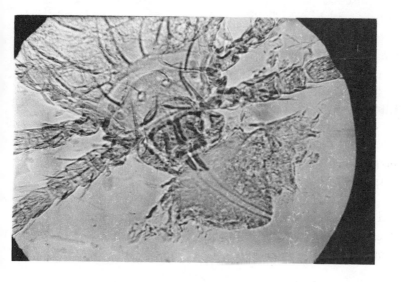

play even worse tricks on the host, for they may actually burrow right into the flesh, where the female will lay its eggs. Intense itching and general ill health result, which reduces resistance to other diseases. They also secrete a poison when they feed that contributes to the itching.

The larva of the harvest mite, or red bug, is called the chigger. Attaching itself to the skin, it gorges itself with fluids and dissolved tissue cells and causes severe itching (red-bug dermatitis). It is encountered more frequently in the southern than the northern portions of the United States.

Should you find you have been in an area infested by chiggers, take a hot soapy bath as soon as possible. If you can do this within an hour, any chiggers you have picked up will be killed before they attach themselves to your skin.

**FLEAS** But the chigger is much less harmful than the chigoe, with which it is sometimes confused. The chigoe is a small parasitic flea found in tropical America and, in earlier times, the southern United States. Humans and domesticated animals tend to be the main hosts. The fertilized female chigoe usually locates on the legs and, boring into the flesh, feeds on the blood, causing a painful infected sore. The chigoe is also called the jigger flea; one wonders whether that refers to the flea or the host.

Fleas are small (about 5 mm. or .2 in.) wingless insects that generally live on the exterior of the host. They have flattened, smooth bodies, which helps them move easily between hair or feathers; this shape also makes it less likely that the flea will be harmed by slapping, pinching, or other physical attacks by the host. A few types, the so-called stick-tight fleas, remain strongly embedded in one position after attaching themselves.

Dog and cat fleas are common in the United States. Dusting the infested animal with insecticidal powder or using a flea collar is the usual method of control. This is important not only for the comfort and

The oriental rat flea *Xenopxylla cheopis*, the major vector of bubonic plague and murine typhus, has been at the core of some of the worst human catastrophes of all time.

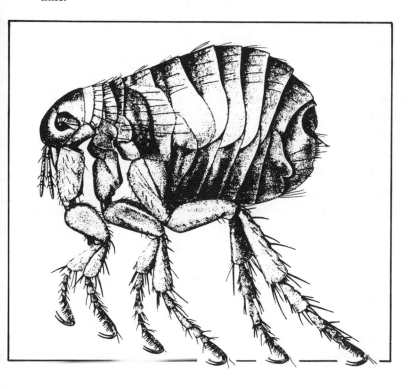

safety of the animal, but because these species, as well as the human flea (*Pulex irritans*, common throughout most of the world) also attack humans. Another species transmits the disease tularemia from rabbits to man, while rat fleas, as we shall see later, have been at the core of some of the major human catastrophes of all time. Fleas and chiggers also transmit typhus, for which, fortunately, effective vaccines are available.

Like other blood-sucking insects, fleas have special piercing and sucking mouth parts. The main one in this case is a thin tube with a saw at the tip to aid in the piercing operation. As the blood is taken in, saliva is injected to keep the blood from hardening before the flea has had its fill; this substance is what leads to the irritation one gets with a flea bite, and also may deliver disease organisms.

In the days before radio and television, small traveling circuses and side shows were an important part of everyone's entertainment. And a common act in these shows—often the whole show—was made up of trained fleas! They pulled tiny cars, waltzed with each other, and did other such tricks. How well trained they were is something of a question. The real trick was setting up the fleas so that they had no choice but to do what was required, like tying a "harness" around a flea in such a way that it could not jump but had to walk and "pull" the tiny cart when the table was jiggled slightly.

They were also "trained" to jump; but this was real, for jump they did—about 50 times their height or length. A human with the same capability could high jump 15–18 meters (250–300 ft.!). The fleas' streamlined, flattened shape, small size, and specially adapted legs give them this ability, which is clearly a very useful way of getting away from danger.

Because they are pests to both domestic animals and humans, fleas are the most familiar insects to most of the peoples of the world—except perhaps for flies.

**FLIES** The number of areas in which flies have found to be troublesome to humans and their pets and livestock is really astounding. Almost anywhere in the world, we are likely to come across one type of biting fly or other. At the extremes of size in this group we have the horse fly, which may have a wing span of five centimeters (two inches) to the tiny punky or no-see-um, which is so small it looks like a dot of black pepper. Though it passes easily through standard window screen and mosquito netting, it can, amazingly, deliver a vicious bite.

Flies have two wings, thus differing from all other orders of insects, which generally have four. The second pair is represented instead by a pair of club-shaped organs called halteres (hal teer′ eez) that act as gyroscopes or balancers. These help to give flies their remarkable flying capability.

No-see-ums, being so small, are often hard to see individually, yet can occur in huge numbers, and their bites usually result in a raised swelling that may itch for several days. If we visit a wilderness area in summer, we are likely to find ourselves tormented by these tiny insects. It does little good to remind ourselves that, like mites and fleas, they are merely looking for a good meal.

Horseflies are very harmful to cattle, the irritation of their bites causing a loss of grazing time—which

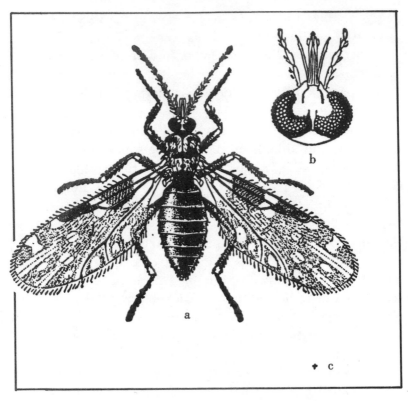

(a) Adult punkie or no-see-um.    (b) Head of a punkie.
(c) Actual size.

means less meat is produced in a given time—and poor
health. While the female horsefly feeds on the blood of
animals, especially cattle and horses, the male feeds on
the pollen and nectar of flowers.

The black fly (1–5 mm. or .04–.2 in. in length) has
a pair of bladelike mouth parts that act like scissors in
reverse, i.e., the cutting edges are on the outside of the
blades. At the same time that these are cutting into
the skin a tube is being inserted through which saliva

is injected (as an anticoagulant) and blood is drawn from the victim.

The stable or dog fly, a vicious biter, may actually account for a serious blood loss in domestic animals. With a related fly, the greenhead, you are actually likely to see blood running down your leg if bitten there! The greenhead is easily recognized by the large iridescent (shiny-colored) eyes that cover most of its head. It prefers moving victims. If there are more than one nearby, try remaining motionless; they may fly away.

While individual blackflies, sometimes called buf-

Black fly has a characteristic "hump backed" appearance.

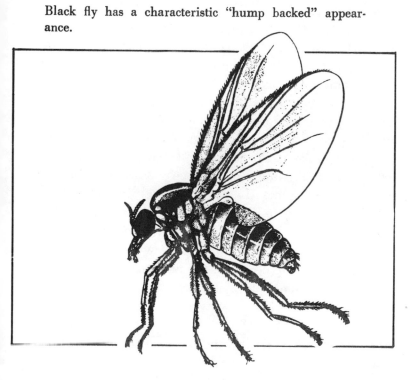

falo gnats, are not large they and some of the other flies occasionally appear in thick swarms. Since each insect is able to bite several times, it is easy to see what can happen to a person caught far from shelter. Explorers, hunters, and fishermen in the northern sub-arctic regions are often caught in this way. These persistent insects will attack along the edges of the hair, on the neck, eyes, ears, and wrists—wherever the hair is short. They will even try to force their way inside collars and cuffs. They readily draw blood and apparently inject a bit of poison as well, for serious attacks cause marked symptoms of poisoning. A number of deaths have been reported from such attacks. The entomologist Brian Hocking reports that "sleigh dogs, still essential to life in many northern areas, at the height of fly-time must dig holes in the ground in which to crouch for protection, and their owners annoint them and themselves with potent mixtures of tar, balsam gum, and lard."

People will sometimes insist that they have been bitten by the standard housefly. Actually the culprit was probably the stable fly, for the two insects look very much alike. A closer look will show that the mouth parts are quite different, however. As shown in the drawing, the stable fly has a sharp, stiff proboscis, which is lacking in the housefly. Like horseflies, the stable fly breeds in dung and straw. Happily, it is far less common today than in the past, when horses were found in large numbers. But the flies may also breed in any kind of damp, decaying organic matter, such as grass cuttings, straw, grain waste, and seaweed. Thus they may sometimes be found in large numbers on southern beaches. A drawing of the housefly's mouth-parts can be seen on page 117.

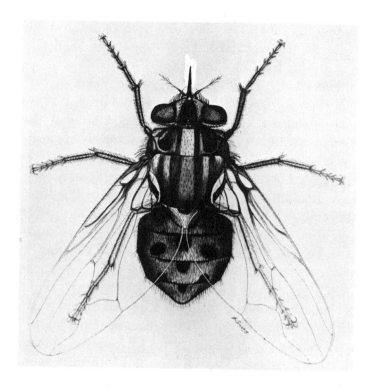

Stablefly (stomoxys calcitrans), top view. Note strong
biting proboscis.

Sometimes the bite of a fly does more than irritate;
it may be the transmitter of a wide variety of diseases.
Some, like anthrax and filariasis (also called elephantiasis), are relatively well known. Others, like Loa loa or
"eye worm" and Phlebotomus (sand fly) fever, are less
well known but still troublesome in various parts of
the world. As we shall see in the next chapter, a disease transmitted by a fly in Africa is so widespread that
this fly, not humans, might be said to be in charge of
large parts of that continent. A number of biting flies,

including the tiny no-see-um, have been found to transmit disease to man and animal. And as we shall also see, nonbiting flies too carry disease.

There are yet other members of the fly family that do not carry infections, that do not even bite, but cause much damage nonetheless. An African relative of the housefly, the hippopotamus botfly, generally deposits its eggs in the body openings of the hippo. Now, remember that most insects do not emerge from their eggs as small adults, as mammals do. Rather they may go through several quite different stages before reaching adulthood. So it is with the fly, and the creature that comes out of the egg is called a larva or maggot. Though it is a soft-bodied, wormlike creature, it eats its way right into the flesh.

Sometimes, however, the botfly makes a mistake and lays its eggs in the nostrils of a sleeping human, particularly one with a cold. If this happens, the human is in trouble. A few days later he is likely to develop a terrible headache; after that his sight begins to go and then disappears altogether. The larvae, using specially adapted flesh-cutting mouth parts, have eaten their way right through the nasal sinuses into his eyes! Something similar happens to animals, such as sheep, causing "blind staggers," loss of weight through irritation, and sometimes death.

Sometimes insects "get together" to do their unpleasant work. The human botfly attaches its eggs to the abdomen of a mosquito. As the mosquito is biting a human, the botfly eggs will hatch and bore into the skin of the host.

Another terrible pest that works in the same way is the screwworm fly, which is a serious scourge of the

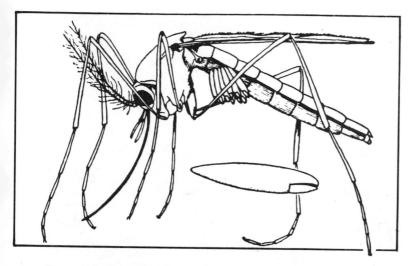

Eggs of human bot fly attached to a mosquito. Enlargement of one egg is seen below the mosquito.

southern cattle industry. Interestingly, a recent survey has shown that 85 percent of the screwworms infesting cattle were located on parts of the animal that were first injured by ticks. Gulf Coast ticks, for example, attach in large numbers to the outer and inner ears of cattle, causing extreme discomfort as well as swelling and sores. The animals rub against trees and posts for relief, often creating or enlarging open wounds. Cattle with deformed ears bring a lower price, and badly infested animals weigh less, which also lowers the price. More serious, however, is the fact that the sores caused in this way are attractive to screwworm flies. Currently, the combined attacks of ticks and screwworms are causing enormous losses to cattle raisers, not to speak of the discomfort of the cattle. The U.S. Department of Agriculture is experimenting with insecticide-

Mosquito biting into an unprotected arm. Note stomach already swollen with blood.

impregnated ear tags as a way of providing the most direct protection possible. A quite different kind of attack on the screwworm fly is in process; we will talk about that in the next chapter.

Now and then one also hears of humans, particularly those with severe colds, being parasitized by the screwworm fly. One researcher, F. L. Washburn, reported seeing maggots of this species taken from a baby's hand that had previously been smeared with a sweet oil. If allowed to remain on the skin, the maggots would have forced their way into the skin.

**MOSQUITOES** Mosquitoes, like flies, are biters, and much of what we have said about the biting habits of flies apply as well to mosquitoes. Mosquito infestations can be so bad that they make some areas of the earth uninhabitable. Though their bite does not contain venom as do those of bees and wasps, some species do transmit disease with their bite. While the bite of tropical species is less annoying than that of the types found in temperate areas like the United States, tropical mosquitoes are more likely to be the carrier of some disease.

Fortunately, there are various treatments for such diseases; but clearly the best approach is to prevent their spread altogether by eliminating the carrier, i.e.,

Mouth parts of a female mosquito: (a) antennae, (b) food tube, (c) saliva tube, (d) sharply pointed stylets for penetration, (e) stylets with teeth at end for cutting, (f) sheath into which (b)—(e) fit for protection when not in use, (g) eye.

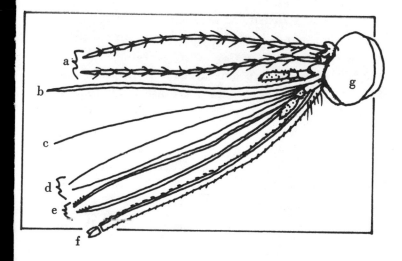

the mosquitoes. This has been done to a large extent in cities such as Havana, Cuba, where yellow fever was at one time a terrible problem, mainly by eliminating any stagnant water where mosquito eggs can hatch and carry on their activities. The brave activities of Dr. Walter Reed and his small band of helpers around the turn of this century, through which the part played by the mosquito was finally discovered, is one of the great medical detective stories of our time.

But outside of cities, it has proved impossible to kill off all mosquitoes. As one worker from the New Jersey Agricultural Experiment Station put it, if you want to prevent mosquito bites, "Avoid going out in the early morning, stay indoors in the late afternoon, and try to stay home in the evening. Assuming your screens are in good order, you should be all right."

Other more serious recommendations are to drain away all standing puddles during the summer breeding season; keep weeds and grass cut short; put goldfish in artificial, standing ponds to eat mosquito larvae as they hatch; make sure that all containers that can hold water (paint cans, discarded tires, old rain barrels) are turned in such a position that the water runs out, or throw them out altogether.

It is also helpful to stay as cool as possible and bathe frequently, as mosquitoes are attracted to perspiration. Sprays are not too effective, except in closed areas. Calamine lotion and other preparations sold in drug stores can help alleviate some of the itch once you have been bitten. A group of so-called electronic mosquito repellers have been put on the market in recent years. These supposedly repel the attacking mosquitoes by mimicking the sound of the bat, the mosquito's main enemy. It's an interesting idea. Unfortunately, according to the Environmental Protection Agency (EPA), they don't work. About 150 mosquito repellents—sprays and ointments—have, however, received approval by the EPA; these are marked "EPA Reg." or "USDA Reg." at the bottom.

As with fly and bee envenomizations, some persons are allergic to mosquito bites, and may develop fever, nausea, and black and blue marks. As with all arthropod envenomizations, any kind of systemic response (general sickness, aches, etc.) should be a sign for medical treatment.

**BUGS**  Bugs, as we noted earlier, are Hemiptera, a group of winged insects with a simple life cycle and piercing and sucking mouth parts. Many of these creatures are venomous. The giant water bug is a murderous creature—particularly in the small-animal world. Up to three inches long, it can both swim and fly, and preys upon birds, snakes, frogs, and fish, as well as insects. Using needlelike hooks on its front legs to keep its prey from escaping, it will sink its beak into the luckless victim and inject its powerful venom, then suck up the victim's blood and dissolved tissues. But if disturbed by a human, it will jab its beak into the human's skin as well. Many people are allergic to the water bug's venom, and severe pain may result. Assassin bugs too can inflict very painful wounds. In South and Central America, a related species, known as the kissing bug, transmits Chagas's disease, which is often fatal; this bug (part of a group called conenoses) is an effective vector because its bite is *not* painful. The blood-sucking conenose is found in the Southwest.

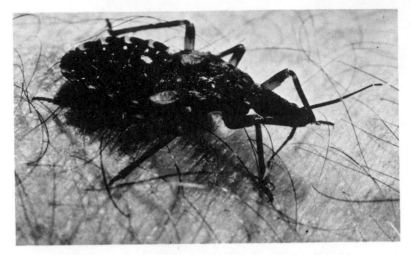

Conenose or kissing bug (Triatoma), which often takes its meal from the human face, is a transmitter of Chagas's disease.

The kissing bug is so called because its meal is sometimes taken from the face, and it is sometimes called the Mexican bedbug because it is often found in houses. But the common domestic bedbug is not a conenose; and it is known more for its desire to share our beds than for the damage it can inflict. The bedbug's bite is normally rather mild, comparable to a mosquito's. Some people do not feel the bite at all, and may find only after-the-fact evidence of its presence in the form of one or more small raised wheals on their skin and perhaps some itching. Certain individuals are very sensitive to these bites, however, and may develop skin and nervous disorders as a result of exposure.

The wheel bug, as shown in the drawing, is an unusual creature, with a cogwheel-like crest on its back.

While, as with most other bugs, this one also preys on insects, it will bite humans if it feels threatened. The bite results in immediate and intense pain which, however, usually subsides in three to six hours even without treatment. Anyone known to be allergic to bug (Hemiptera) bites, though, should seek medical treatment.

**CENTIPEDES AND MILLIPEDES** The common house centipede (*Scutigera forceps*) may look threatening with its strange many-segment, many-leg shape, but it is quite harmless to humans. As a matter of fact it is a useful animal because it feeds on flies and other unwanted insects about the house. It is typically only a few centimeters (about an inch) in length.

In tropical and subtropical areas, however, we find quite another story. In the southern and southwestern portions of the United States, they may reach a length of 15 centimeters (6 in.), while the tropical species may attain a length of 25 centimeters (about a foot!) or more. A bite from one of these can result in

Wheel bug

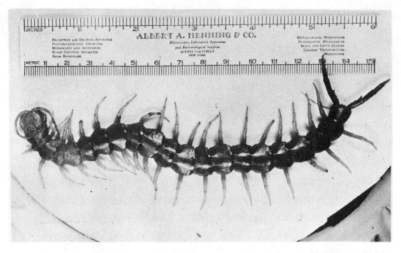

*Scolopendra heros*, a large centipede of the United States South and Southwest, ranges up to about 15 centimeters in length. What appears to be the first pair of legs (at the left) are really its poison jaws, or poison claws, as they are sometimes called.

death. While there have been no fatalities reported from centipede bites in the United States, intense pain can result immediately, with redness, swelling, and a burning, aching pain to follow. These symptoms will usually subside in four or five hours. In rare cases red blotches will appear on the limb that has been bitten.

During the day, centipedes tend to hide in dark, moist, and otherwise protected locations. They come out at night to hunt for prey which usually consists of insects or other arthropods. When they catch something, they inject their venom through two powerful claws in the under part of the body just behind the head.

When you are camping in an area that is known

to contain such centipedes, it is wise to invert, shake out, and inspect shoes, sleeping bags, and anything else that comes in contact with the ground. Always wear shoes when walking around at night. Remember that centipedes are more interested in food than in you and will tend to bite only when accidentally picked up, stepped on, or trapped inside some article of clothing that you put on.

If you are bitten, first aid is usually all that is necessary. This will include washing the wound with soap and water; applying a solution of one part ammonia to nine parts water; applying cool, wet dressings of a strong magnesium sulfate solution; taking pain-killers when necessary.

Millipedes ("thousand legs") are sometimes mistaken for centipedes, which they resemble to some extent. But they have two pairs of legs per body segment, and are much slower moving. Some millipedes have openings in the skin through which they emit a vesicating venom that can cause injury to a person handling them. Some (e.g., *Rhinocricus*) are able to squirt a vesicant some distance; it can cause severe injury if received in the eye. Millipedes will sometimes invade a home in great numbers.

**SPIDERS** Spiders may be the most feared of all arthropods. Perhaps it is because of their strange, often hairy, bulbous bodies and their menacing appearance. Perhaps it is because the bite of some species does not need the more indirect route of disease or allergy to cause death. (While some scorpions are similarly dangerous, as a group they are far less familiar to most of us, and so are less threatening.)

As we know, a spider is not an insect but an

arachnid. It has eight, not six, legs, a two-part body, no wings, and no antennae. The head, however, has a pair of antennalike organs called pedipalps and a pair of fangs that are connected to the spider's poison glands. Those two contribute to the fearsome reputation of this arthropod.

But human skin is a fairly tough material and the truth of the matter is that few spiders have fangs that can penetrate it, most spider fangs being either too short or too weak; and the venom of those which can penetrate can usually produce only local symptoms or an occasional allergic reaction. Thus, although spiders are among the most fearsome-looking of the arthropods, most are quite harmless to humans. This includes the large, hairy tarantula, the very name of which is enough to send shudders down the spines of many people. One store owner who has been robbed several times put one in his window each night, along with a sign: "This store patrolled by tarantulas." The robberies ceased.

Another particularly scary creature is the giant bird-eating spider of South America, which attains a length of 5 centimeters (2 in.). With its 18–centimeter (7–in.) leg-span it is capable of rapid movement. It, and the black, hairy tarantula may scare one to death (which no doubt accounts for the many accounts of their supposed deadliness), but their bites are relatively harmless, at least to humans.

Many people have apparently begun to realize this, and a number of collectors have begun to purchase tarantulas as pets, for among the more sophisticated nature lovers, they are known to be docile. And of course, the shock value of being able to show one of them off is very tempting.

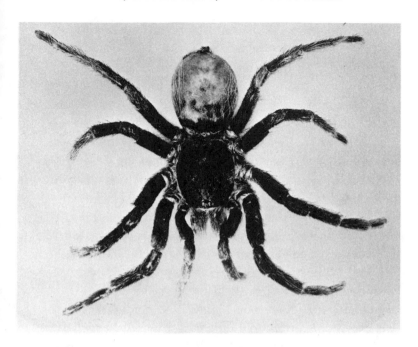

Tarantula

But as Dr. Ralph E. Crabill, Jr., of the Smithsonian Institution in Washington, D.C., explains: "I myself don't like to see the public buying tarantulas as pets unless they can be awfully sure of what the thing is and where it comes from. Who knows where these suppliers get them? I'm personally pretty leery of the whole idea because there are tarantulas and there are tarantulas. Those occurring north of Mexico, however ferocious looking and big, are apparently perfectly harmless. Mexico and the Caribbean have some that are pretty dangerous, however; and in South America, some are exceedingly dangerous. It takes an authority to make a confident identification. So you can see the potential problem."

An interesting example of this problem is seen in the fact that one species of tarantula that sells very well is an attractive type decorated with red bands. Unfortunately, when annoyed it will use its rear legs to flick hairs from its body at the intruder; these have been found to be nettling hairs and can create a very aggravating skin condition if treatment is not received in time.

If any of the more dangerous species escapes, as often happens when they are in the care of amateurs, they could conceivably establish themselves and begin to breed in the United States, although generally tropical animals do not do well in cooler, drier areas.

There are, however, a few U.S. spiders that are extremely dangerous to humans. It would be well for you to become familiar with their appearance. This is particularly true of the black widow and brown recluse spiders. Interestingly, it took a long while to sort out the true from the exaggerated stories. Indeed, early investigators made some serious mistakes. In 1899, a Russian team was sent out to determine whether the bite of the *karakurt* ("black wolf," actually a black widow spider) was really dangerous to humans. Time after time the experimenters tried to get live specimens to bite them, but without success. (Perhaps the shy creatures were too frightened?) After a number of attempts, they concluded that the stories about the venomous *karakurt* were not true.

One of the members then decided to take some pictures to show this. He placed six of the spiders on the bare chest of a man and started to take the pictures.

Suddenly one of the spiders darted down the man's arm and bit him on the hand. In a few minutes the victim was trembling violently, his eyes were dull, and his face showed an expression of great terror. Half an hour later he had convulsions and cramps and began to vomit and sweat profusely. There was severe pain, and even though he fell unconscious, he cried out in pain. This subject seems to have been lucky and to have survived the experience. But some 4 or 5 percent of untreated bites result in death due to the powerful action of the venom on the central nervous system. An antivenin is available which can help prevent serious illness and death.

There are still conflicting reports on how dangerous certain spiders are. One important reason for the confusion has to do with the fact that the poison sac of spiders is surrounded by muscle, and when the spider strikes it may or may not inject venom; the amount it injects may also vary. But any bite of these spiders is potentially dangerous. One symptom is a rigid, tender abdomen, the same symptom as results from appendicitis and peritonitis. Cases are known of people who were operated on unnecessarily because of such a misdiagnosis.

It is the female black widow that one must avoid; the male is both smaller and truly harmless. The female sports a shiny black body, is about 1.5 centimeters (0.6 in.) long, and usually has an hourglass-shaped marking on the underside of her rounded body that is usually red, but may be orange, cream, or some other color. The shape of the marking may also vary somewhat and may even be composed of dots, triangles, or other forms. The male, in addition to being smaller, is

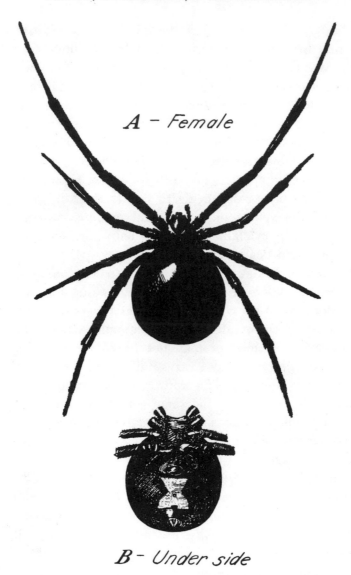

*A - Female*

*B - Under side*

Black widow spider. Note hourglass marking on underside of female's abdomen.

usually of a patterned brown color. This spider is called the black widow because of the female's rather interesting habit of occasionally eating the male after mating.

The technical name for the species is similarly descriptive. *Latrodectus* is derived from *latro*, a robber, and *dect(o)*, biting. *Mactans* is a Latin word for murderous. Hence we have *Latrodectus mactans*, a murderous biting robber; not a bad description. Though the black widow is found throughout the continental United States, most deaths caused by this spider have occurred in the Southeast.

*Latrodectus* tends to build loose webs in wood piles, cellars, basement windows, and cool outbuildings like the old-fashioned privy. With the gradual elimination of this type of building, some of the opportunities for black widow/human run-ins have happily been decreased. On the other hand, with increasing amounts of land being ploughed under and forests cut down, the black widow has been forced out of her natural habitat and has moved into wood piles, barns, and other places frequented by humans. So we come out about even.

The brown recluse (*Loxosceles reclusa*), on the other hand, seems to be expanding its territory. Originally found almost exclusively in the south and south-central states, it is now found in some northern areas as well. There are several reasons for its expansion. This spider prefers warmth and quiet. In the southern states it can get this in the open. With increasing mobility of Americans, more of these spiders accidentally find themselves in other areas. Normally they would die out, being very sensitive to cold; but with central heating, which sends heat to all parts of a house, they live very nicely in warm closets, attics, and cellars, or behind pictures, catching their occasional insect, until happened upon by some luckless human. Warehouses and vacation homes (unused for large parts of the year) are other favorite spots for the brown recluse.

Both male and female brown recluse spiders will bite, rather than just the female, as in the black widow. And the results are somewhat different from a black widow bite. Killed tissue is the typical reaction. The victim may or may not be aware of the bite at first and may or may not have an immediate reaction; perhaps there will be a stinging sensation. This is normally followed by intense pain. A blister will develop and a large area around the bite will become swollen. The victim may become feverish and restess. Gradually the tissue around the bite dies and falls away, leaving a crater-shaped depression, often the size of a half dollar and deep enough to expose muscle tissue. This may never heal properly and skin grafting may be necessary. In one case, a bite on a man's thumb caused a reaction all the way up his arm. The venom can also affect the kidneys and in rare cases may cause death.

The spider is about the same size as the black widow but has longer legs, with about a 20 to 40 millimeter (0.8 to 1.6 in.) leg-span. Its color ranges from yellow tan to dark brown, and it has six eyes (most spiders, including the black widow, have eight). And, finally, it has a violin-shaped marking on the back of its forward section.

There are other types of *Loxosceles* spider. Though dangerous enough, the *reclusa* form is not the most venomous of the group. This distinction belongs to

Female brown recluse spider. Note characteristic violin-shaped marking on front half of its back.

*Loxosceles laetae,* a South American type that has gained entrance into the United States a number of times. Several communities in Los Angeles County, California, have recently reported that fairly large numbers of this type have been found in these areas. The reason for concentrating on the recluse in this book is that it is far more common in the United States—its range being stated as central Illinois to the Gulf Coast, and from Oklahoma and Kansas to Georgia. It has also been reported in Ohio, New Jersey, and Wyoming. But it is probably safe to say that the genus *Loxosceles*, in one form or another, is found all over the continental United States.

If you are hypersensitive to bites and stings of any kind, it might be worth contacting a doctor for desensitizing shots. But the best approach, as always, is to be careful, especially when poking about in little-frequented areas. If possible, do not camp near rock piles or fallen trees; spiders, and scorpions as well, often hide in such places. It is also worth noting that a bite or sting in an arm or leg is likely to be less dangerous than one in the neck, for if the bite is on the neck, the venom may interfere with breathing or paralyze the vocal cords.

In general, if a nonallergic person is stung or bitten by a venomous insect, remove the sting if there is one, and apply ice or cold water; this will slow chemical activity in the area. If the victim begins to show any systemic signs, such as wheezing, abdominal pain, fainting, shortness of breath, or generalized swelling, a doctor's services should be sought immediately. Similarly, if a scorpion or known-to-be-venomous spider is the culprit, get medical help right away. Put the victim's hand or foot in ice water until help is available. Care should be taken in so doing, however, as there is a possibility of damage to the victim's tissues.

If a spider is the cause, it is well to know what type it is. Capture it, dead or alive, if you can. You may save the victim considerable fear and worry. There are many spiders that look like a black widow, for instance, and whose nip may feel no better or worse than a real black widow's bite. It will hurt for a while, but is no more troublesome than any other typical insect bite.

# 5 DISEASE CARRIERS

From red-bugs and bed-bugs, from sand-flies and
    land-flies,
  Mosquitoes, gallnippers and fleas,
From hog-ticks and dog-ticks, from hen-lice and
    men-lice,
  We pray thee, good Lord, give us ease.

                          (An old prayer)

A few years ago lice were discovered in the scalps of a number of children in the local elementary school. There was near hysteria. The children were sent home immediately; their shame was deep and everyone was accusing everyone else of being the cause. One girl still washes her hair every day and sometimes twice a day.

Infestations like this are not uncommon, and even seem to be on the rise. Itch mite infestation, for example, is still frequently seen in hands in some parts of the world; it therefore spreads easily in hospitals and office buildings, where hand-shaking is common.

But plague, pestilence, and pus caused by arthropods were far more common even half a century ago. A book written in 1914 (*Insects Injurious to the Household*) devoted six full pages in the "itch mite of man." Further back, lice were sometimes equated with manliness and in some cases with saintliness!

Over its past history, humankind has been subject to a vast variety of such visitations, and worse. We little appreciate the debt we owe to soap and hot water as well as to chemicals and medical drugs. Disease, much of it insect borne, was said to have wiped out several times as many of our colonial soldiers as did the British. In a book called *Rats, Lice, and History,* which has become something of a classic, Hans Zinsser wrote that "again and again, the forward march of

**113**

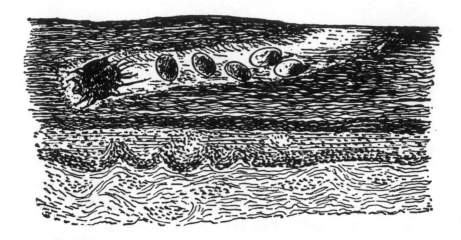

Itch mite tunneling

Head louse

[ancient] Roman power and world organization was interrupted by the only force against which political genius and military valor were utterly powerless— epidemic disease." Napoleon's disastrous retreat from Moscow, after the apparently successful invasion in 1812, was probably due as much to louse-borne typhus as to the severe Russian winter. At the end there were only 30,000 survivors; more than 500,000 men had been lost. And we shall shortly learn of other such catastrophes.

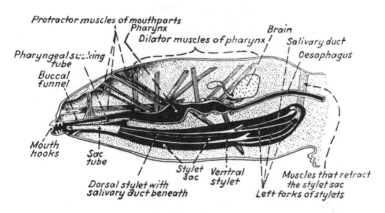

Mouth parts of louse

Suppose, then, one were to ask, what is the most dangerous arthropod in the Western Hemisphere? Would you say the black widow spider? The scorpion? African bee? Not at all. If a single species had to be chosen, it would probably be the common housefly, at least in the United States. For while spiders, scorpions, and bees can cause death by bites and stings, the number of deaths is relatively few. But the house fly does its

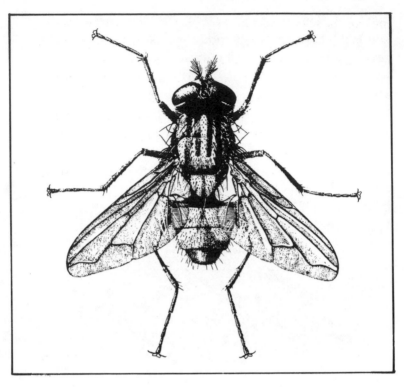

Housefly

dirty work everywhere. And though it does not bite, the list of diseases it carries and spreads includes many of the worst killers of mankind—typhoid, cholera, gangrene, tuberculosis, gonorrhea, bubonic plague, leprosy, diphtheria, scarlet fever, amoebic dysentery, poliomyelitis, and many others. (Suddenly, using a hornet's nest to help keep a house free of flies doesn't seem like such a bad idea.)

Because it does not bite and inject the infecting microorganism, the fly is called a "mechanical carrier" of disease. Others are caterpillars, beetles, ants, and cockroaches. The microorganisms that flies carry generally get into our systems through our mouths, mostly when the flies, having picked them up from some diseased source, deposit them on food when they feed, which we then take into our bodies. Most of these infecting organisms thrive in a warm, moist environment with lots of good food to eat, which is just what they find in our digestive systems. They multiply and invade other tissues, destroying them or messing up their

The housefly adds insult to insult. When it feeds on garbage or other contaminated material, it may pick up disease-causing organisms both with its pad-like sucking mouthparts (left), and its feet (right). The feet have both claws and hollow hairs that secrete a sticky liquid, which is how it is able to walk upside down. When the fly lands on uncontaminated food, it therefore dirties the food with both its mouth and feet.

activities in some way and, presto, we are sick. There are perhaps 200 species of these "domesticated" flies, of which the most important are the common housefly, the stable fly, and certain blowflies (including the bluebottle fly, with its shiny blue body).

But many diseases are also spread by biters. And these are sometimes far more troublesome—for the same reason that medical shots are more effective, and work faster, than pills. In other words, the organism carried by a biter is injected directly into the blood stream, which is constantly being circulated through all parts of the body. Thus if a microorganism happens to attack nerve tissue, there need be no time wasted. Very shortly it will be carried to nerve tissue directly and can immediately start its dirty work. Thus this "system" works much faster than mechanical transmission.

The result is that the disease may spread with incredible rapidity. This is pretty much the definition of the word *epidemic*. The problem is likely to be particularly serious if the disease is brought from a distant part of the world to a place where it has not been experienced before. Here's why.

**THE BODY'S DEFENSE SYSTEM** As you probably know, the body is not totally helpless when invaded by germs. Each of us has a built-in defense system—several, in fact. One of the most effective of these defense systems requires some sort of previous contact with the infecting agent, against which it can then custom-build antibodies. Antibodies are specific substances in our bodies which act to kill or neutralize the disease agent. If these antibodies are already in our system—from a successful earlier bout with a disease, say—we can fight off a direct injection of the germs into our blood stream, as might be the case when we are bitten by an infected mosquito. If we do not get sick at all, we are said to be immune to the disease.

But if the disease is new to our area, our antibody-building system must start right from the beginning, and it takes time for the antibodies to be built. If the infection does its work faster than we can build antibodies, or faster than our bodies' other systems can attack it, the result may be very serious illness. If our defense systems manage to catch up, we get well again; if they are evenly matched, the result is a kind of chronic, or steady, illness; and if our defenses are completely overwhelmed, the result may be death.

What kind of a useless system is this, you may wonder, if it doesn't have all the antibodies already built in for all the disease organisms in the world? There are two answers to this not unreasonable question. First, just as a carpenter or builder needs plans to build from, so too does our antibody-production system need a pattern for the different types of disease organisms, also called pathogens, against which it must protect us. This can only come from some sort of contact with the specific pathogens.

But, just for the sake of argument, let us assume that the proper mixture of antibodies *is* present in our defense system. The problem is that disease agents are generally living microorganisms—bacteria, protozoans, viruses,* and the like. These are small and multiply very rapidly when conditions are right.

---

* Some people might argue that viruses are not alive in a true biological sense. The question is interesting but need not detain us here. The point is that they act like living things, particularly with respect to disease.

Now nature has built into all living things the ability to change or mutate. Not that each individual can change its biology (as opposed to habits), but the species can, over the course of time, actually change. Thus the horse of today is not the same as the horse of a million years ago; a human today is not the same as the human of a million years ago.

Disease organisms change too. But because these are very small and multiply very rapidly, their opportunities to change or mutate are much greater than ours. Therefore, even if we had been provided with antibodies against every disease organism now in existence, the set would be outdated in a few years. So having each type of antibody custom made turns out to be a very good idea.

But rather than take a chance on the first natural contact being gentle enough to give the production system a chance to work, medical researchers have developed the system called immunization. In this method a small, controlled amount of (sometimes weakened) pathogen—a virus in the well-known case of smallpox vaccination—is introduced into the body, against which the system can then build immunity.

Nor is our defense system the only pathogen killer. All living things—including infectious microorganisms—have their enemies. It is known, for example, that a dog or cat will often show no effects from a dose of *Salmonella* bacteria that would make a human extremely sick. Researchers believe this is because of other organisms contained in the animals' bodies, but not in ours, that kill off the pathogenic bacteria.

Often, just the fact that the disease is around means that everyone has had some contact with it—

some more and some less, of course, but at least some contact. It is in the air, so to speak, and so there is time for antibodies to be produced or perhaps for anti-pathogen organisms to develop in the potential victims' bodies.

**MOSQUITO-BORNE DISEASE** Malaria, yellow fever, dengue (deng′ gee), filariasis, and encephalitis are important diseases transmitted by mosquitoes, mainly by the *Culex* (common house mosquito), *Aedes,* and *Anopheles.* The accompanying table shows which of the types transmits which diseases. Although use of insecticides has greatly reduced the hazards of malaria, it is still responsible for two million deaths a year. Because of its continuing importance, we discuss it separately in the next section.

Yellow fever, similarly a killer, is today confined to Africa and to Central and South America. Dengue, an infectious virus disease characterized by severe pains in the head, eyes, muscles, and joints, is found in tropical and subtropical regions, including (until recently) the United States. It is not usually a killer, but is important because of its rapid spread.

Filariasis, mentioned earlier in connection with flies, is an infestation of the blood or tissues by tiny threadlike nematodes (worms) which are injected into the blood when the victim is bitten by an infected fly or mosquito.* It is a serious problem in tropical and subtropical regions. The World Health Organization reports that at least 200 million people worldwide are

---

* Technically, a mosquito is a type of fly.

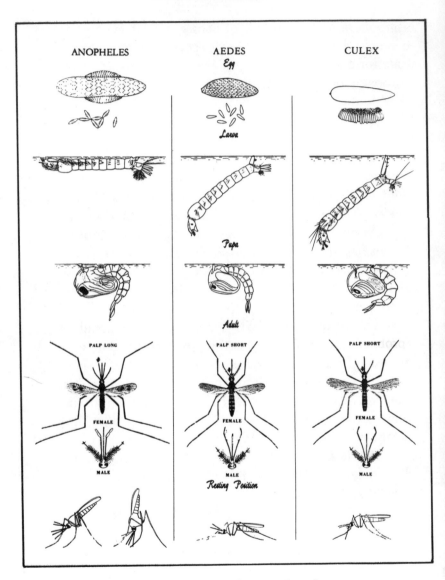

Three important mosquitos and stage of each

infected with one form or another of this parasitic disease. Two forms of it may result in the seriously disfiguring condition known as elephantiasis.

Encephalitis, also due to a virus, is a very serious disease; it attacks the central nervous system and is sometimes fatal. In 1975 an outbreak of the so-called St. Louis type occurred in southern New Jersey; 29 persons were stricken and one died. A different form, called eastern equine encephalitis, is even more dangerous. That is, a person getting this second type is even more likely to die; indeed the mortality (death) rate may run as high as 85 percent. Of those who survive, many have their central nervous systems so damaged that they can no longer function normally. Another type affects about 100 children a year in the midwestern and eastern portions of the United States. There are no known cures for the disease, which is also a problem in Asia.

## COMMON MOSQUITOES AND THE DISEASES THEY TRANSMIT

| CULEX (common house) | AEDES | ANOPHELES |
| --- | --- | --- |
| Filariasis Encephalitis | Dengue Yellow Fever Filariasis Encephalitis | Malaria Filariasis |

**MALARIA** The malaria situation in Africa is very serious. And it is all the more sad because in at least some of the trouble areas, the disease has been intensified or even brought in as a result of attempts to improve a different problem. In a poor region of Guyana, villagers tried to change from production of maize (a kind of corn) and cassava, which they could eat but could not sell, to rice, which is a more marketable crop.

The major problem is that the rice fields have to be kept very wet. This has provided lovely breeding grounds for mosquitoes, particularly the *Anopheles aquasalis*, which is the vector for malaria. Normally this species prefers the blood of cattle and oxen, which had once been abundant, while the mosquitoes had not been. Now the situation is reversed, for rice and livestock do not mix, and in clearing the area for the rice, the cattle and oxen that had been kept were displaced. And so the mosquitoes have turned to another ready source, human blood. The result has been a disastrous rise in malaria.

Robert Desowitz describes this sad situation in an article in *Natural History* (October, 1976). He points out that introduction of rice growing may also change the type of mosquito in an area from mostly non-malarial to malaria-bearing. He adds: "Similar alterations in mosquito populations following the introduction of rice farming have occurred in such diverse areas of the world as Venezuela, Tanzania, India, Syria, and Morocco, where until 1949 the French colonial government had, for health reasons, banned rice growing."

He also points out that rain forests do not, contrary to what we might expect, act as good mosquito breeders, for there are few standing pools of water (it is rapidly soaked up by the rich vegetation). And the *Anopheles* mosquitoes prefer sunlit breeding areas.

Clearing these forests for farmland therefore also provides improved breeding areas for these troublesome insects.

Interestingly, in some cases the reverse takes place, as in the introduction of the cacao industry in Trinidad. (Cacao is the source of chocolate and cocoa.) Planting of immortelle trees, used to provide the shade needed by the cacao plants, again improved the breeding situation for the Trinidad *Anopheles* mosquito. What happened was that a type of plant called a bromeliad epiphyte grew on the high immortelle trees and collected water in small natural containers where the leaf stem joins the stalk. It turns out that these mosquitoes breed only in these containers. They proliferated and carried malaria to the plantation workers and their families. We shall see later that attempts at chemical control of the mosquito are often doomed to failure. The reasons are complex, fascinating, and disquieting.

In another approach to economic development, Third World governments in underdeveloped areas have also tried to institute or increase production of electric power through the building of dams and hydroelectric plants. But dams turn running water into standing water. In addition, there is seepage from the large lakes and reservoirs, with the same results we have already discussed. Even where the dams were not directly the cause of trouble, they often disrupted established patterns and again caused an increase in malaria. The huge deforestation program carried out in Viet Nam by the United States had a similar effect, with the result that American soldiers were severely affected.

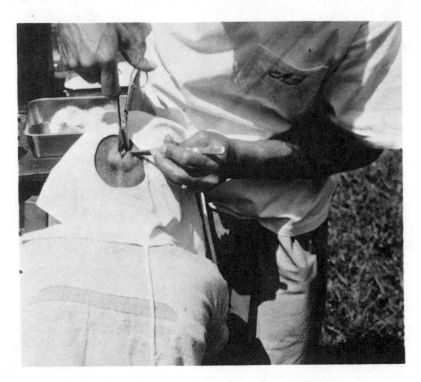

Surgery (in Guatamala) to remove from a patient's scalp
a nodule of parasites that cause river blindness. The
microfilariae (baby worms) of this parasite migrate
through the tissues of the body, causing blindness if they
reach the eye.

**CURRENT STATE OF AFFAIRS** Unfortunately, even
some of the progress that has been made in Africa has
been wiped out by the current unrest. Thus malaria is
returning in stronger force; a million children die there
each year due to this one disease. Other diseases are
also troublesome. In parts of Central Africa, Central
America and northern South America, river blindness,

carried by several species of black fly, leaves tens of thousands of persons sightless each year.

Another biter that has had a huge impact on the development, or lack of development, in Africa is the tsetse fly, which we discuss in the next section.

**SLEEPING SICKNESS** In thinking about disease, we tend to be single-minded. The disease should be wiped out, we feel, and that's all there is to it. But things aren't always that simple. A good case in point is sleeping sickness, found only in Africa because the vector (the tsetse fly) is found only there (though fossils forms of this insect have been found in Colorado!) Sleeping sickness affects both humans and hoofed animals, including cattle. Until late in the 1800s it was confined to a small region of West Africa, largely because intertribal warfare kept the inhabitants in their separate areas.

European colonists in Africa had rather good success in putting an end to this warfare. As a result, there was considerably more travel between territories, and the disease has spread widely; fortunately, it remains confined to that continent.

Sleeping sickness is caused by a trypanosome, a protozoan blood parasite, which is transmitted by the bite of the tsetse fly; the disease is therefore also called trypanosomiasis (trih pan oh so my' uh sis). The tsetse fly is somewhat larger than the American horsefly.

A human struck by this disease grows increasingly tired and apparently lazy, sleeps more and more, eats less and less, and, if not treated, will die.

Oddly, the most important aspect of the disease, to the Africans, is not that it causes death in humans, which it does, but that it prevents inhabitants from

Tsetse fly biting

keeping cattle; the point is that cattle are not only used for food but are to the Africans what jewels and fine clothes are to us—outward signs of wealth.

Combined attempts to stamp out the disease in both humans and cattle have, on the whole, been more successful with the cattle form, with a resulting large increase in the cattle population. To a poor nation, this would seem at first a boon. Yet any population can become too large in the sense that it begins to outstrip the capacity of the environment to carry it. In the case of cattle, increased production may lead to overgrazing—eating the vegetation faster than the land can grow it. In areas like the Kalahari and northern Namibia, soil erosion has become a great problem. We see here and elsewhere the continuing replacement of relatively productive land with unproductive desert. And once the process begins, it is most difficult to reverse.

But the problem is a complicated one and not easy to pin down. When such destruction of soil takes place,

Africa's cattle raising country and tsetse infested areas show virtually no overlap. Tsetse caused disease has kept four million square miles of grazing land out of production.

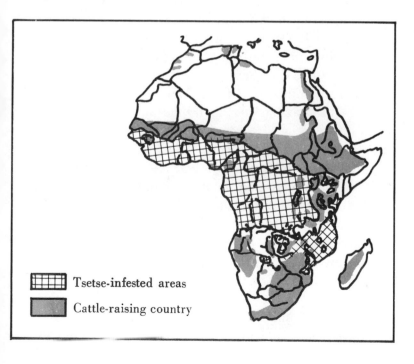

Tsetse-infested areas

Cattle-raising country

it is likely to be over a large area and can easily be blamed on natural forces such as large-scale changes in weather, natural wearing out of the land, and so on, rather than overgrazing.

The overgrazing argument goes like this: more cattle mean more wealth; more money, along with disease control, leads to increased holdings of other animals such as sheep and goats; larger holdings lead to more strain on the vegetation; pressure on the plant life of the area leads to more desertification; and desertification, say some climate specialists, can itself cause a decrease in rainfall!

This decrease has to do with the fact that desert reflects more sunlight back to the sky than does a grassy or tree-filled area. There have been several serious droughts in the last couple of decades, the last one (end of the 1960s and first half of the 1970s) was a particularly serious and long lasting one. W. E. Ormerod, of the London School of Hygiene and Tropical Medicine, predicts in *Science* Magazine: "Unless the pressure of grazing on the fragile savannah regions south of the Sahara is eased, greater droughts will occur at more frequent intervals."

An associated problem is that increased cattle production, and increased human population, will put increasing pressure on the wild game animals—elephants, zebras, giraffes, and so on—which have acquired a natural immunity to the disease, having lived for millions of years with the trypanosome that causes it.

All of this is not to say that control of the tsetse fly should not be attempted, but rather to show the tremendous, if indirect, effect that an insect can have on the economic and social characteristics of a country.

**OTHER ARTHROPOD-BORNE DISEASES** In South
America a different form of trypanosomiasis is found.
There it has the name Chagas's disease, and is transmitted not by a fly but, as we noted in Chapter 4, by
"kissing bugs." Trypanosomes reproducing in the hind
gut of such a bug are deposited on the skin of the
victim in its fecal material. In other words, it adds insult to injury by defecating on its victim as it feeds.
Because the bug is about an inch long, the trypanosomes are about that far away from the break that the

Laboratory reared (uninfected) kissing bugs (in box on
child's arm) feeding to help detect presence of the typ-
anosomes that cause Chagas's disease. As can be seen
from the relatively untroubled expression on the child's
face, the bites are not painful.

bug makes in the skin. If it is washed off or dries in place, no infection results. But if it is smeared, trouble is likely. If the fecal material is deposited on mucous membrane (e.g., skin of the eyelid, mouth or nostrils), the trypanosomes can invade the body even if there is no break in the skin.

The common effect of Chagas's disease is a long-lasting infection rather than death. But the heart muscle is often involved and it is not unusual for a young person apparently in the prime of life to die suddenly from this heart damage. In some parts of Brazil one-third of adult deaths are caused by Chagas's disease, which gives us an idea of how many people get it each year. It has been suggested that the great Charles Darwin, who suffered in his later years from a strange, incurable illness, may have been a victim of Chagas's disease, probably from an encounter with one of these bugs during one of his research expeditions.

There are other, lesser known diseases, all transmitted by insects, that we have not room to discuss in detail here. One is leishmaniasis, caused by a protozoan injected by the bite of a sandfly. Another is babesiosis, a strange malarialike disease marked by fever and tiredness, which is transmitted from wild rodents through ticks to humans. Formerly rare in humans, it seems to be on the rise, with several cases recently reported on Nantucket Island in New England. In the summer of 1977, five cases were reported on the eastern tip of Long Island. Thus far it has only affected people in the late 40s and above.

Soft ticks, on the other hand, transmit tick-borne relapsing fever. Intermittent bouts of fever, often for several weeks, is the usual course of the disease.

# VECTORS OF HUMAN DISEASE

| VECTOR | DISEASE | SPECIFIC AGENT |
|---|---|---|
| Class **DIPLOPODA** | | |
| Millipedes | Hymenolepiasis | *Hymenolepis dimunata* |
| Class **CRUSTACEA** | | |
| Copepoda (water fleas) | Diphyllobothriasis | *Diphyllobothrium latum* |
| | Dracontiasis | *Dracunculus medinensis* |
| | Gnathostomiasis | *Gnathostoma spinigerum* |
| | Sparganosis | *Diphyllobothrium* spp. |
| Decapoda (crayfish, crabs, etc.) | Paragonimiasis | *Paragonimus westermani* |
| Class **ARACHNIDA** | | |
| Mites | Bertelliasis | *Bertiella studeri* |
| | Rickettsialpox | *Rickettsia akari* |
| | Tsutsugamushi | *Rickettsia tsutsugamushi* |
| Ticks | Boutonneuse fever | *Rickettsia conori* |
| | Bullis fever | *Rickettsia* sp. |
| | Colorado tick fever | Filtrable virus |
| | Encephalitis, Russian spring, summer | *Erro sylvestris virus* |
| | Louping ill | Virus sp. |
| | Maculatum disease | *Rickettsia* sp. |
| | Plague | *Pasteurella pestis* |

# VECTORS OF HUMAN DISEASE (Continued)

| VECTOR | DISEASE | SPECIFIC AGENT |
|---|---|---|
| | Q Fever | *Coxiella burneti* |
| | Relapsing fever (endemic) | *Borrelia duttoni* |
| | Spotted fever | *Rickettsia rickettsia* |
| | Tularemia | *Pasteurella tularensis* |
| **Class INSECTA** | | |
| Black flies | Onchocerciasis | *Onchocerca volvulus* |
| | Tularemia | *Pasteurella tularensis* |
| Cockroaches | Amebiasis | *Endamoeba histolytica* |
| | Balantidiasis | *Balantidium coli* |
| | Cholera | *Vibrio comma* (*cholera*) |
| | Dysentery, bacillary | *Shigella* spp. |
| | Food poisoning | *Staphylococcus* sp. |
| | | *Salmonella* sp. |
| | | *Streptcoccus* sp. |
| | Giardiasis | *Giardia lamblia* |
| | Gongylonemiasis | *Gongylonema pulchrum* |
| | Hymenolepiasis | *Hymenolepis diminuta* |
| | Poliomyelitis | Virus types 1, 2, 3 |
| | Paratyphoid fever | *Salmonella* spp. |
| | Typhoid fever | *Salmonella typhosa* |
| Conenose bugs | Trypanosomiasis (Chagas's) | *Trypanosoma cruzi* |

# VECTORS OF HUMAN DISEASE (Continued)

| VECTOR | DISEASE | SPECIFIC AGENT |
|---|---|---|
| Deer flies | Loaiasis | *Loa loa* |
| | Tularemia | *Pasteurella tularensis* |
| Eye Gnats | Conjunctivitis | Bacteria spp. |
| | Tropical ulcer | Mixed bacteria & spirochete |
| | Trachoma | Virus flora |
| | Yaws | *Treponema pertenue* |
| Fleas | Dipylidiasis | *Dipylidium caninum* |
| | Hymenolepiasis | *Hymenolepis diminuta* |
| | Plague | *Pasteurella pestis* |
| | Typhus fever (endemic) | *Rickettsia mooseri* |
| House fly and other filth flies | Amebiasis | *Endamoeba histolytica* |
| | Bacillary Dysentery | *Shigella* spp |
| | Balantidiasis | *Balantidium coli* |
| | Cholera | *Vibrio comma* (cholera) |
| | Cysticercosis | *Taenia solium* |
| | Food poisoning | *Staphylococcus* sp. |
| | | *Salmonella* sp. |
| | | *Streptococcus* sp. |
| | Giardiasis | *Giardia lamblia* |
| | Paratyphoid fever | *Salmonella* sp. |

## VECTORS OF HUMAN DISEASE (Continued)

| VECTOR | DISEASE | SPECIFIC AGENT |
|---|---|---|
| | Poliomyelitis | Virus types 1, 2, 3. |
| | Trachoma | Virus |
| | Trichuriasis | *Trichuris trichiura* |
| | Tropical ulcer | Mixed bacteria & sprochete flora |
| | Typhoid fever | *Salmonella typhi* |
| | Yaws | *Treponema pertenue* |
| Lice | Relapsing fever (epidemic) | *Borrelia recurrentis* |
| | Trench fever | *Rickettsia quintana* |
| | Typhus fever (epidemic) | *Rickettsia prowazeki* |
| | Brills disease | *Rickettsia prowazeki* |
| Mosquitoes | Dengue | *Charon* sp. virus |
| | Encephalitis | |
| | California | |
| | Equine, Eastern | |
| | Venezuelan | |
| | Western | Virus |
| | Japanese B | |
| | Russian, spring-summer | |
| | West Nile | |
| | Filariasis, Bancroft's | *Wuchereria bancrofti* |
| | " Malayan | *Brugia malayi* |

| VECTOR | DISEASE | SPECIFIC AGENT |
|---|---|---|
| | Malaria | Plasmodium spp. |
| | Myiasis | Dermatobia hominis |
| | Rift Valley fever | virus |
| | Tularemia | Pasteurella tularensis |
| | Yellow fever | Charon evagatus |
| | Tropical (pulmonary) | Dirofilaria imnitis |
| | Eosinophilia | Brugia pabangi |
| Moths & beetles | Hymenolepiasis | Hymenolepis diminuta |
| Biting gnats | Acanthocheilonemiasis | Acanthocheilonema perstans |
| | Mansonelliasis | Mansonella ozzardi |
| | Microfilaria streptocerca | Acanthocheilonema streptocerca |
| Sand flies | Bartonellosis | Bartonella bacilliformis |
| | Espundia | Leishmania brasiliensis |
| | Kala-azar | L. donovani |
| | Oriental sore | L. tropica |
| | Sandfly fever | Pappataci virus |
| Tsetse flies | Trypanosomiasis | Trypanosoma gambiense |
| | | T. rhodesiense |

*Medical Entomology. U.S. Department of the Navy, Naval Medical School 1968*

**PLAGUE (THE BLACK DEATH)** The accompanying table summarizes a lot of the material we have been discussing in this chapter. Buried in that table is a single word, *plague* (under "Fleas" and also under "Ticks," a less common carrier). The term, if you have heard it, probably has a suggestion of something un-pleasant—a plague of locusts, for example. But unless you know something of the history of the disease it-self, from which the more general term comes, you could never imagine that it has been the cause of some of the most incredible disasters ever to strike the hu-man race. (Indeed the term derives from a Latin root meaning, "to strike"; in later times it was referred to as divine justice.)

The full name for the most common form is bu-bonic plague, the bubonic part referring to the *buboes,* or swellings that appear under the arms or in the groin. It is essentially a bacterial disease of rodents, primarily rats, which is transmitted by the oriental rat flea. The flea is therefore said to be the vector of the disease, for the flea will also bite humans and pass the disease on to them. Conditions that foster the existence of fleas and rats—poor sanitation, unwholesome and in-sufficient food (which weakens people's resistance to disease in general), and bad ventilation—also are, for obvious reasons, connected with the disease.

But for unknown reasons, bubonic plague has, at various times in the past, broken out among humans with explosive fury. The worst epidemic, also known as the Black Death, occurred in the middle of the fourteenth century, devastating Europe, Africa, and Asia. It claimed a third of the population of Europe —at least 25 million persons!—over a period of about three years. It struck again, in epidemic form, numerous times in various parts of the world, but never again with the same intensity.

Even during the Black Death, however, some areas, interestingly, were less affected than others. For example Ireland was much less heavily afflicted than England. And Scotland might have been spared altogether had not the Scots invaded England, trying to take advantage of the chaotic conditions there. Not only was the Scottish military force destroyed by the plague as much as by the English, but the survivors brought it back to Scotland with them.

The first major epidemic of the plague to be carefully described took place in the second year of the Peloponnesian War (430 B.C.), seriously weakening ancient Athens in its struggle against the Spartans. The association of the disease with rats was strongly suspected almost from the first. But the connection with fleas was not made until many centuries later. The final demonstration took place in 1907 and was based on a simple experiment. Two groups of disease-free rats were hung at different distances above cages containing plague-infected fleas. These fleas cannot jump higher than 10 cm (about 4 in). One group of rats was hung closer than 10 cm above the fleas and did contract the disease, while the other group was hung more than 10 cm away from the suspected carriers and remained free of it.

This simple but elegant proof that bubonic plague is transmitted by fleas has resulted in measures (including rat control) that can control the disease when and where applied. But the disease can also be gotten from handling a dead rodent and getting infected blood into a cut or abrasion. There are usually two to six cases per year in the United States, though not simultaneously. The disease can spread so quickly that the U.S. Public Health Service considers two simultaneous cases an epidemic!

Though plague is still a problem in some areas of the world, the terrible epidemics of the past are, we hope, also a thing of the past.

# 6 INSECTS VS. MAN

The brontosaurus had a brain no bigger than a crisp,
The dodo had a stammer and the mammoth had a lithp,
The awk was just too awkward, now they're none of them alive.
Every one, like man, had shown himself unfit to survive.
Their story points a moral, now it's we who wear the pants.
The extinction of these species holds a lesson for us—ants.

Michael Flanders, *Dead Ducks*

Insects, as we now know, are a source of everything from irritation to devastation. Clearly, they intrude in our lives; but is it not also true that we are a pain in the thorax to them?

For there are far more of them than there are of us; they inhabit many more regions than we do; and they got there first. Indeed the two oldest forms of animal life appear to be cockroaches and scorpions, both several hundred million years old, compared with humans' paltry one or two million years.

And while mankind seems to have little trouble wiping out larger animals, he has had little success against insects. If a direct confrontation ever takes place between humans and the animal world, it will be with the insects. As a matter of fact, that confrontation may be taking place right now.

For thousands of years humans and the harmful insects were at a kind of standoff, and it was hand-to-hand combat almost all the way. In the ancient city of Cyrene (on the northeast coast of what is now Libya), citizens were required to fight locusts several times a year by going out into the fields and crushing them. Throughout history farmers and gardeners have physically picked insects off crops and plants and killed them by hand. In another interesting early attempt at insect control, officials of the Catholic Church tried excommunicating the offending insects. To the best of our knowledge, the insects ate on

Seeing what wine could do to people, someone in the late Middle Ages suggested trying it on insects. Wine sediment was poured onto the roots of trees which were being attacked by insects, apparently without much success. In the seventeenth and eighteenth centuries powdered tobacco and nicotine made by soaking tobacco leaves in water were tried. While the material had some effect on insects and did not harm plants, nicotine is a dangerous poison to animals.

But there are substances in nature, as we have already noted, that do appear to repel or harm insects. And here we begin to see a more useful approach. Perhaps best known is pyrethrum, a substance produced from the flower of a chrysanthemum plant. Although it is quite effective, it is found only in Southeast Asia, and during World War II, shipments to the United States were cut off. Chemists were able to create synthetic pyrethrums, however. Rotenone, which can be obtained from various plants, began to be used in the mid-1800s to help control leaf-eating caterpillars. And there are other natural substances as well. Some are more effective than others, but all are expensive and not really practical for widespread use.

Knowing what we now do about the damage insects can inflict on humans, not to speak of their crops and domesticated animals, it is not surprising that some of the attempted remedies became rather extreme. It was known, for example, that most insects can be killed by heat, say 50° C (122° F) for several minutes. One approach that was tried was to close all windows in a house on a hot summer day and build up all the fires as high as possible. Unfortunately, it takes time for the heat to penetrate into bedding, wood floors, and the like. And while there are known cases of this method's being 100 percent successful—it was only because the house burned down!

With the beginnings of modern chemistry, a new approach began to take shape, for chemists began to create new substances in the laboratory, substances not seen in nature before. An arsenic compound called Paris green was used to control the Colorado potato beetle in the 1860s. Arsenic compounds also kill plants, however, which did not make the farmers happy.

But this new chemical approach, called synthesis, opened up a totally new era in human existence—for good and bad—and has had an enormous effect on our lives. A vast range of new materials has been synthesized by chemists.

Sometimes the materials find immediate and widespread use. Plastics, for instance, are used in clothing, buildings, drugs, furniture, automobiles, and household products, and they have many other useful and helpful applications. New drugs and medicines have saved millions of lives. But sometimes a substance results that seems to have no use at all.

In 1874, a substance with a quite unpronounceable name was synthesized. In this case the chemical, called dichlorodiphenyltrichloroethane,* just sort of sat around doing nothing until the 1930s—when it was finally found to have insect-killing properties.

Perhaps you have already recognized it as the now famous DDT. And it is famous for good reason. While the word brings forth as many negative reactions

---

* The long name is used for a reason; in dealing with it, chemists know immediately what the material consists of.

as positive ones, its early successes seemed little short
of miraculous. During World War II, many thousands
of civilian Italians were probably saved from a typhus
epidemic when DDT replaced rotenone for control of
body lice. That was the first major war in history in
which fewer soldiers died of communicable (catching)
diseases than by military action. After the war, use of
DDT on flies, mosquitoes, fleas, and lice throughout the
world is credited with saving millions of lives that
would otherwise have been lost due to malaria, yellow
fever, plague, and other such diseases.

**PESTICIDE PROBLEMS**  Other, similar insecticides began to be developed. One of the main advantages of
these substances seemed to be their persistence. A
house could be sprayed once and the treatment lasted
for months and perhaps years. It really looked, for a
while, as if the battle against insects had been won.
U.S. farmers were able to increase their production by
10 percent in the following decades just by use of the
new pesticides, which also acted against rats, birds,
and other crop eaters.

But the materials, it finally began to be realized,
could not distinguish between pests and nonpests, and
they killed nondestructive creatures as well. Even
worse, they killed insects and animals that originally
preyed upon many destructive insects!

Further, the persistence of DDT, which at first
seemed such an advantage, eventually spelled its doom,
at least in the United States. For, beginning even in
the 1940s, traces of the substance began to be found
in the tissue of fish, animals, and humans. The problem
was that when it did not kill outright, it tended to be

stored in the fatty tissue. And due to the way of life in the wild, it became more and more concentrated in certain animals' tissues.

For example, a bird may eat many insects over the course of its life. And while the DDT in each insect might not be enough to kill either the insect or the bird, it would remain in the fatty tissue of the bird, adding to whatever amount was already there, finally building to lethal concentrations.

The "cure" in many cases therefore turned out to be worse than the disease. There were numerous fish kills, bird deaths, and more subtle effects as well. DDT was found to be affecting the shells of bird eggs, preventing the young from hatching properly, and eventually causing a decline in the numbers of several much admired birds—ospreys, bald eagles, peregrine falcons, and brown pelicans. *

Other types of pesticides were developed which were less persistent—which, in other words, were broken down more easily in the course of nature's workings; but these have had other drawbacks. One widely used group, the organophosphates, have proved to be a highly dangerous substance for farmers and their families. At least 150 deaths, many of them of children, occur each year from exposure to insecticides,

---

* There are some researchers who argue that the pesticide argument is overemphasized, that hunting and other people-connected practices do far more damage to wildlife than pesticides, and finally, that if not for pesticides a great deal more land would have to be put into agriculture, thus cutting further the land available for trees and wildlife. (See for example, "Eagles, Affluence and Pesticides" by A. J. Rogers, *Mosquito News*, June 1972, pp. 151-157.)

mostly from the organophosphates. Parathion is another important killer of humans. In 1967, 17 persons died and more than 600 became ill when flour contaminated with parathion was accidentally used for bread in a Mexican village. Part of the problem is carelessness, part is ignorance, and part is simply the danger of handling dangerous materials. These figures, then, must be added to the toll that insects take of human life.

**BUGS STRIKE BACK** And now, as if that were not enough, the bugs are striking back. First, some species have actually developed immunity to many of our strongest insecticides, and a few, including some malaria-carrying mosquitoes, have become resistant to all known insecticides.

The reason is not far to seek. We think that all insects within a given species are alike. But no, they do indeed have variations; and among these variations is resistance to insecticides; some are more resistant than others. Let us say a field is sprayed with DDT and 90 percent of a certain group of harmful insects are killed. The remaining 10 percent can then reproduce without competition from their own species and with practically no competition from their natural enemies, many of which have also been killed. As we noted earlier, insects have an incredible reproductive capacity. It is said that if the offspring of a single pair of flies could reproduce without environmental resistance, they would in a single season cover the earth in a layer several feet thick. Another example is that of the queen termite which can lay some 6,000 eggs a day for 15 years. The result is that larger and larger amounts of insecticide must be used to accomplish the same results.

Female dog tick depositing eggs

Furthermore, it has been found that chemicals can cause mutations in animal life. The outcome may be the development of characteristics that are even more threatening than those of the original insect. Strains of cabbage maggot that are resistant to the insecticide cyclodiene have been found to lay twice as many eggs and have twice the lifespan of nonresistant strains!

It may also be that larger insects are at a disadvantage under normal environmental conditions, which is undoubtedly why (happily) most insects are small. But when these conditions are disturbed, and widespread spraying of insecticides is certainly disturbing, we may find that larger insects—or smarter, or more venomous ones—may well be the overall result. A species of grasshopper is said to have incorporated insecticides into its body chemistry in such a way as to make it repellent or dangerous to its normal enemies. One hesitates to imagine the results if this should start happening among venomous arthropods. They would be using our own poisons against us! It should be kept in mind too that insects in prehistoric times sometimes attained incredible sizes—a species of dragonfly found in the United States having had a wing spread of 76 centimeters (30 in.)!

And, finally, the economics of the situation must be considered. While new chemical pesticides are continually appearing on the market, the cost of research and development is high. Many substances must be carefully tested before one is found to be usable, practical, and within cost bounds. In 1970, for example, about 63,000 chemicals were screened for use as pesticides, and of these only 11 were finally registered for release on the market. Normally it takes five years for a company to evaluate, test, develop, produce, and begin marketing a new pesticide.

But in the meantime, remember, the insects are finding their own ways of battling back. And with their short reproductive cycle, needed change (needed from their point of view) can occur fairly rapidly, and a whole generation of resistant insects can appear in a very short time.

In at least one case, this proved the ruination of a carefully controlled experiment. A group of researchers tried to determine scientifically whether flies were actually spreading acute diarrheal infection among children in a region of Mexico. The towns within the region were divided into two groups, one of which was sprayed with DDT to get rid of the flies, while the other was not. As expected, in the latter towns the rate of infection remained unchanged, while in the treated towns it dropped.

This was a good indication, but was not conclusive; and after a year and a half the towns were to be reversed. In other words, the untreated towns were to be sprayed and the treatment discontinued in the treated towns. Sure enough, when this was done, a reversal of the rates of infection seemed to be occurring. But before the experiment could be completed, the flies in the towns being treated developed a strong resistance to the DDT, and the experiment had to be discontinued.

In a major study on pest control, the National Academy of Sciences revealed that despite the wealth of talent and energy the chemical companies have thrown into the battle against insects, the insects are growing increasingly resistant to the chemical approach. During the past 50 years, more than 200 arthropod species have developed resistance to the chemicals. The head of the study, biologist Donald Kennedy of Stanford University, says the efficacy of the chemicals is "decreasing alarmingly."

The social insects may prove to be the greatest challenge of all. With the fire ant, for example, we already saw that things have gotten so bad in some places that farm laborers have refused to work in certain fields. The owners, as a result, have abandoned some of these fields to the ants. Not without a struggle, I must add.

But we are not dealing here with mosquitoes in a house where, with patience, they can be tracked down and killed with a fly swatter or by closing the windows and spraying the whole house (which I would hesitate most strongly to do).

No, here we are involved in a struggle that is more difficult by a whole order of magnitude. In one early battle against the fire ant, *Solenopsis*, when pesticide experts were brought in, they decided to use dieldrin. This insecticide, which had been tested on *Solenopsis* in the laboratory and found to be very effective, was then sprayed, under pressure, into the mounds. It killed off many of the ants, but the mound remained in operating order!

One of these mounds was then carefully opened and investigated. The researchers discovered that no sooner had spraying started than the young, defenseless ants had been carried through an underground maze to a safe place! Unfortunately, this powerful poison killed off practically everything else in the area.

Fumigants, which act more quickly than dieldrin,

Fire ants scurry to protect their queens as a shovel is thrust into this multiple queen mound. Entomologist Clarence E. Stringer records their movements for study.

were tried, with no better success. Chauvin, the ant
expert, reports: "And—peak of perversity—the workers
return to the nest afterwards and enlarge the openings
as if they sought to air it. A few days later the whole
tribe is triumphantly reinstalled."

Poisoned bait was tried. This had somewhat more
effect. But somehow the young fertilized queens, which
had burrowed underground because of the above-
mentioned treatments, remained there without eating;
by the time they had produced a new generation of
workers, the poison bait had lost its strength or had
been washed away by rain.

Another chemical, Mirex, was finally found to be
useful in the fight. Mixed in small quantities with
soybean oil and corncob grits, it seems to kill only ants.
They drag the bait back to the nests and the whole
colony is wiped out.

But the ant is so widespread that in order for an
eradication program to be effective, it was felt that the
bait had to be spread by airplane and ground equipment over large areas. To date some 200 million acres
of southern soil have been treated in this way.

As the program has gone on, however, environmental and health hazards have begun to surface. The
National Cancer Institute reports that studies indicate
Mirex causes cancer in laboratory animals, and small
amounts of Mirex have been found in about one-quarter
of human tissue samples taken in the South. It also
seems to be breaking down in the ground into the toxic
pesticide Kepone, which was recently implicated in a
disaster where employees in a plant making Kepone
were found to be suffering from severe nervous system
disorders. And the persistence problem has arisen

In federal-state fire ant control programs using Mirex in Mississippi and eight other infested states, hand treatments are used in areas not suitable for aerial programs such as those containing navigable rivers or water used for human consumption. Also, mounds that survive aerial application must be killed by hand treatments to prevent rapid repopulation of treated areas.

again: Mirex is one of the most persistent pesticides in existence; after ten years, half the original amount remains active.

As a result, widespread spraying has been stopped, and as of 1978 the material must be phased out altogether. The problem is that no other substance has been found that will work anywhere near as well. The question that must be asked, however, is, how serious is the disease? Once again, the cure has been found to be worse than the disease.

In examining the effects of these chemicals on nontarget species, the National Academy of Sciences came up with essentially the same conclusions we have already considered, but added a frightening fact: "The pest control enterprise places a billion pounds of toxic materials into the environment each year, but it is 'normal' for us to have only the vaguest idea of how much of each compound was used and where, and even then only after half a decade's lag." The report calls for a major change in the way industry reports its procedures.

It has been found, in a recent California report, that due mainly to use of these chemicals, agriculture is the most dangerous occupation in the state!

**NEW APPROACHES**   These problems have not, of course, gone unrecognized by agricultural and chemical scientists. And several different kinds of weapon are being thrown into the battle or are in the experimental stage. These fall under a grouping generally called biological, or bioenvironmental, control. Biological control can be as simple as changing a planting schedule to pull a crop's cycle out of mesh with an insect's. Or it can be as complicated as some of the ones we mention below.

a) Chemicals from the laboratory are being developed that mimic insects' chemicals and interfere with the reproduction and/or development of the insect. The objective is not to poison the

pests with what are essentially chemical block-
busters but to affect the highly specific processes
that are unique to a certain insect, thus leaving un-
affected other animal life, including humans.

At the International Center of Insect Physiology and Ecology in Nairobi, Kenya, a group of
scientists is deeply involved in the dead-serious
fight against insects. In one experimental procedure, a chemical hormone is being used that has
been found to interfere with the ability of the
tsetse fly to reproduce.* One unusual way to get
it to the flies is to feed it to the cattle! Because
the substance is basically an insect hormone, the
cattle should not be affected, but flies that bite
them will automatically take in a dose and become
unable to reproduce. A similar approach is being
tried with a hormone that affects ticks, preventing
them from molting, or shedding, their old, out-
grown skin. They will then die before they can
reproduce.

Insects both give off and respond to chemical
compounds called pheromones. These regulate the
activities rather than the physical development of
the insects, and they have already been used to
lure insects into traps where they can be killed or
counted for study purposes. In another demonstration, beetles became so confused that they lost
their nesting and mating instincts and left the
area.

But even here a problem must be faced.

---

* A hormone is a chemical compound that regulates the
growth, development, or reproduction of an organism.

Broad-scale insecticides (pesticides) are economically attractive to develop precisely because they are broad scale and hence find wide use, i.e., against many different types of insects. But if a substance is finally developed that is active against the kissing bug, and the kissing bug only, how much can the developing company expect to sell? Even if the government pays the cost of development, it may not pay for a company to get involved.

**b)** We can try to use other living things that are natural enemies of the insect we are attempting to control or eliminate. These can involve parasites, predators, and microorganisms such as viruses and bacteria that produce disease in the offending insect and only that organism. It was only two years ago (1976) that the first virus was cleared by the Environmental Protection Agency for field use, in this case against the cotton bollworm and the tobacco budworm. It is indicative of the real-world situation that the first such substance turned out to be for use against a farm pest rather than a deadly bug or killer insect.

Gardeners who purchase preying mantises or ladybugs for use against back-yard pests, rather than spraying, are casting their vote for this method.

Research at the Insects Affecting Man Research Laboratory in Florida has shown that that major pest, the housefly, can be controlled without use of pesticides through use of a tiny wasp (*Spalangia endius*). As shown in the photo, large numbers of the parasitic wasp are released in heavily

Entomologist Philip B. Morgan prepares a wasp release station at a 4,200-chicken egg production house which is infested with house flies. A quarter of a million of the tiny *Spalangia endius* wasps will be released per week from six release stations over a period of ten weeks.

infested areas. The female wasp seeks out a fly pupa, drills into it with her ovipositor or egg depositor (which is the "proper" use of a sting), deposits one egg on the developing fly, and at the same time feeds a bit on the blood of the fly that emerges from the wound. When the egg hatches, the developing wasp uses the fly pupa as food, thus killing it. The wasps do not bother humans or animals and will remain in the infested area as long as there are flies to feed on. If they perform too effectively, they either die out or leave. In a test at a calf barn at a commercial dairy, fly control was about 90 percent effective within a month, and all of the fly pupae collected in the study were found to be parasitized.

c) We can increase the resistance of desirable plants and animals (I guess that includes us) against pests. Long-standing techniques are already available for doing this in plants and animals; newer ones based on new discoveries in genetics may make it possible to do the same for humans—if it should ever become necessary.

d) We can develop and use improved repellents and perhaps attractants (to lure undesirable insects to their death in traps). Another approach under investigation is to impregnate clothing with repellent or even insectide that kills, say, mosquitoes on contact. Current repellents are more or less effective against mosquitoes, biting flies, gnats, chiggers, fleas and ticks. They are not effective against wasps, spiders, and scorpions.

e) Pests can be sterilized by radiation or chemical treatment. In one of the more successful approaches to specific pest control, the screwworm fly was eradicated in a section of the Southwest by raising and sterilizing great numbers of male screwworm flies, then releasing them in the affected area. As it happens, females of this species mate only once. When a sterilized male mates with a female, no offspring result, and that female is then effectively out of commission. If enough sterilized males are released they can in effect "use up" the reproductive capacity of that generation, and the final effect is to wipe it out. The method, though expensive, has worked in several areas.

f) If we put all these methods together into an overall scheme, called "integrated pest control," we can make the greastest use of natural control and the smallest possible use of harmful chemicals.

One interesting experiment in integrated pest management combines chemical control and the sterile male technique in an attack on the horn fly, which invaded the United States about 1890 and causes a loss of many millions of dollars each year in the livestock industry. If uncontrolled, 3,000 or more of these bloodsucking pests may attack one cow, cutting the milk output by a fifth, and reducing weight gains of beef cattle. In this experiment, a chemical called methoprene, which is an insect growth regulator, was added to the drinking water of cattle. As in the tsetse fly example given a few pages back, the material is an insect growth regulator and so has little or no effect on the cattle; yet it effectively reduces the adult population of the horn fly. This prepares the way for the release of sterile male horn flies which mate with the remaining fertile females. These then lay eggs which fail to hatch, further reducing the horn fly population.

Adding the chemical to the water instead of applying it to the skin of the animal, which has also been tried, has the following advantages: (1) The cows do not have to be rounded up for treatment, and (2) the sterile males released later do not die from contact with any insecticide still remaining on the cattle before they have a chance to mate.

The importance of these five methods (a–e) lies not only in the fact that only the offending insects are affected, but also in that the insects are much less likely to be able to develop resistance to them.

A further fact to keep in mind is that most insecticides are made from petroleum, and we shouldn't have to be reminded of both the cost and potential scarcity problems associated with that raw material.

## MAKING INTEGRATED PEST MANAGEMENT WORK

Now, integrated pest management is clearly a good idea—especially for a well-equipped laboratory where the researchers may have time to think things through carefully and carry out relatively complex procedures. But tailoring insect-fighting programs to fit specific farm situations is obviously a far more complicated procedure for farmers than simply spraying insecticides at fixed intervals, the usual approach on farms. It is hoped that simpler data-gathering procedures, which can be combined with computer technology, can provide farmers with the kind of information they would need to make integrated pest management work.

Orchard owners in Michigan, for example, are being offered an experimental "dial-a-bug" service. Information is being collected on 27 different regions throughout Michigan and fed into computer terminals for analysis by a central computer. Information on crop management needs is then developed and passed on to government agricultural agents who record the proper telephone message for each region. In a comparison between owners who do and do not use the system, it was found that use permitted a 30 percent reduction in the amount of pesticide used, with no reduction in yield. Aside from the general benefits of pouring less insecticide into the ecosystem, savings on this increasingly costly material more than make up for the costs of monitoring the orchards and running the computer. While the economics of this situation may not yet make it useful for deadly bugs and killer insects, it is clear that whatever is learned about farm pests will be useful in the fight against all other arthropods.

**A LOOK AT THE ENEMY**  Just what kind of an enemy are we battling? How smart are insects? Individually they are not smart at all; but somehow, as a group (particularly the social insects), they can be credited with a remarkable variety of accomplishments, such as keeping slaves and maintaining complex social arrangements, with queens, workers, and soldiers all doing their jobs. They build incredibly complicated nests and keep them in good repair. Again, this seems to be a societal, not an individual, capacity.

On the other hand, there is new evidence that a capability humans had once reserved for themselves as a purely human trait—the making and use of tools—actually exists in the insect world.

It had been known for quite a while that chimpanzees strip small branches of leaves and poke the resulting stick into ant and termite mounds. The in-

A string of tropical army ants forms a ladder for use by others.

sects "attack" the intruder (the stick), which the chimp withdraws and then uses as a "popsicle stick," these insects being considered a delicacy by the animal.

Now it has been discovered that ants too make and use tools, a discovery that has stunned scholars in the field. Some kinds of ants use tiny bits of leaf, mud, or grains of sand to help them carry more food back to the nest on each trip than they could using their natural methods. In essence, they dip the bits of material in liquid food and carry the food that way. In so doing, each ant is estimated to be able to carry 10 times more food than it could hold in its crop (part of the intestine). It is believed that development of this method helps certain less aggressive species compete with more dominant species, in that they need spend less time at a food source.

What kind of enemy are we fighting, indeed? Fleas and many other insects, for example, can survive in hot dry deserts or inside the Antarctic Circle. In that cold, inhospitable climate, they may lie frozen in ice and snow for as long as nine months each year. As a matter of fact the number of mosquitoes per unit area is probably ten times higher in the Arctic regions than in any tropical area of the world. Though the female mosquito needs human blood for its egg-laying phase, mosquitoes live mainly on plant juices. During warmer periods in the Arctic, the top two inches of land melts but the water cannot seep down because of the permafrost below. The result is hundreds of square miles of excellent mosquito breeding grounds.

Insects are, in other words, well equipped to withstand difficult periods, while their great diversity enables one species or another to fit just about anywhere on earth.

Entomologist R. E. Pfadt tells us that the three most significant features of insects are:

1) their small size, which allows them to live in sites too small for many other animals and which permits them to flourish on small quantities of food,

2) their short life cycle, which makes it possible for them to complete a life cycle in sites that are livable only a short time, and

3) their great mobility, particularly their ability to fly, enabling them to travel to favorable sites and avoid adverse conditions.

We have already discussed a few cases where one species will drive out another. And we have seen that some farmers in the United States have abandoned their fields to the fire ant.

But it is in the tropical and semitropical areas that the real battle will take place. In South America there is an insect called *chirimacha*. Four times the size of the common housefly, it thrives on garbage and kitchen leftovers, can live for months without food or air, and, as an extra added attraction, carries Chagas's disease. In one section of Peru, composed mostly of slum areas, the infestations were so bad a couple of years ago that the government stepped in to try to get rid of them. But the *chirimacha* came out the victor, partly due to its fantastic reproductive capability, and partly to the fact that it has become, or perhaps has always been, immune to pesticides. Finally, the residents were forced to leave their homes and move away from the humid valley in which they were living to the cooler, drier mountains. The *chirimacha* would probably disappear if the slums could be eliminated. Until then, the area remains in their "hands."

INSECTS VS. MAN

How bad can things get? Legend has it that a magnificent city called New Tarrangona, once the proud capital of New Andalucia in Venezuela, was attacked in the seventeenth century by huge red ants. The ants invaded the fields first and destroyed crops. Then the city itself came under attack—with young people and the elderly being killed in attacks. The ants undermined buildings, some of which collapsed, and established bases in almost every building.

The people of New Tarragona fought back with the few weapons they had. Normally such an infestation would reach a peak and then die away. But this did not seem to happen. At last the people just started moving away, first a few and then more and more. At last the city was given over to the ants. The dense green jungle, once held at bay by the people of the city, closed in. The last account of life in New Tarragona was written in 1690.

Is there any likelihood that we shall have to abandon Macon, Georgia, to the fire ants, or Tucson, Arizona, to killer bees? Not very likely; but you never can tell. Some extraordinarily dangerous mutant strain of insect might arise.

But beekeepers in the northern part of South America, where Africanized bees have moved in, tell of numerous battles between these bees and army ants on the move.

So maybe, if things get bad enough, we can just get out of the way and let the ants and bees fight it out.

At the moment, happily, we can reserve such a scenario for a bad horror movie. There is no question, however, that if we should let down our guard, or if war, starvation, or other disaster should strike, no

Entomologist Douglas C. Ferguson selects specimens for study from the more than 24 million insects stored in 58,000 drawers in the National Insect Collection. Scientists at the laboratory identify from 250,000 to 350,000 insect and mite specimens that are sent in each year. Without accurate identification, costly mistakes can be made in control measures, medical treatment, or quarantine procedures.

mutant will be necessary to create a disaster. The existing arthropods will once again advance in strength.

It is important to understand, in other words, that our fight against insects will be an ongoing one. It is most unlikely that the ultimate weapon will ever be found, for the insects are continually developing new strains that enable them to cope with each new threat to their existence.

Similarly, the once-current approach of trying to exterminate completely a particular insect pest is no longer considered sensible. Integrated pest management tries instead to establish some sort of balance, hoping to prevent any single insect species from becoming a serious problem.

New ideas and new workers are constantly needed in this challenging field. With the ever-growing resources of modern science and technology—and less grandiose ideas of what can be accomplished—we may be able to stop polluting our earth with pesticides, and yet still stay ahead in the battle against the arthropods.

# Suggested Readings

## BOOKS

Arehart-Treichel, J., *Poisons and Toxins*, Holiday House, 1976.

Askew, R. R., *Parasitic Insects*, American Elsevier, 1971. (Advanced.)

Bouvier, E. L., *Psychic Life of Insects*, Century, 1922.

Brown, D., *Tales of the Warrior Ants*, Putnam, 1973.

Bucherl, W., Buckley, G., and Deulofen, V., eds., *Venomous Animals and Their Venoms*, Academic Press, Vol. 1, 1968; Vol. 2, 1970; Vol. 3, 1971. (Advanced.)

Burt, D. R. R., *Platyhelminthes and Parasitism*, American Elsevier, 1970. (Advanced.)

Burton, Maurice, *Encyclopedia of Insects and Arachnids*, Crescent Books, 1975.

Bush, G. S., *The Strange World of Insects*, Putnam, 1968.

Busvine, J. R., *Insects, Hygiene and History*, Humanities Press, 1976.

Caras, Roger, *The Venomous Animals*, Barre, 1974.

Caras, Roger, *Venomous Animals of the World*, Prentice-Hall, 1974.

Chauvin, R., *The World of Ants*, Hill and Wang, 1971.

Clausen, L. M., *Insect Fact and Folklore*, Macmillan, 1954.

Cloudesley-Thompson, J. L., *Insects and History*, St. Martin's Press, 1977.

Crane, Eva, ed., *Honey: A Comprehensive Survey*, Crane, Russek, 1975.

Fabre, J. H. C., *Insect World of Henri Fabre*, Dodd Mead, 1949. (Classic.)

Fichter, G. S., *Insect Pests,* Golden Press, 1966.

Friedlander, C. P., *The Biology of Insects,* Pica Press, 1977.

Gregg, C. T., *Plague! The Shocking Story of a Dread Disease in America Today,* Scribners, 1978.

Hellman, Hal, *The Right Size,* Putnam, 1968.

Herrick, G. W., *Insects Injurious to the Household and Annoying to Man,* Macmillan, 1914.

Herzog, Arthur, *The Swarm,* Simon & Schuster, 1974.

Howard, L. O., *Insect Menace,* Century, 1931.

Jacobson, M., *Insecticides of the Future,* Dekker, 1975.

James, M. T., and R. F. Harwood, *Herms's Medical Entomology,* Macmillan, 6th ed., 1969. (Advanced.)

Linsenmaier, Walter, *The Insect World,* Odyssey Press, 1964.

McKelvey, J. J., Jr., *Man Against Tsetse,* Cornell University Press, 1973.

McMillen, Whealer, *Bugs or People?* Appleton, 1965.

McNeill, W. H., *Plagues and Peoples,* Doubleday, 1977.

More, D., *The Bee Book. The History and Natural History of the Honeybee,* Universe Books, 1976.

Morse, R., *The Complete Guide to Beekeeping,* Dutton, 1974.

National Geographic Society, *Our Insect Friends and Foes and Spiders,* National Geographic Society, 1935.

Neider, Charles, ed., *Man Against Nature,* Harper, 1954. (Especially Tursa, "Buzzing Death," pp. 452 ff.).

Newman, L. H., *Man and Insects; Insect Allies and Enemies,* Natural History Press, 1965, 1966.

Pfadt, R. E., *Fundamentals of Applied Entomology,* Macmillan, 2nd ed., 1971. (Advanced but readable.)

Potter, S., *Killer Bees,* Grosset and Dunlap, 1977.

Rau, P., and Rau, N., *Wasp Studies Afield,* Dover, 1970.

Ricciuti, E., *Killer Animals,* Walker, 1976.

Rood, Ronald, *It's Going to Sting Me!,* Simon & Schuster, 1976.

Smith, J. B., *Our Insect Friends and Enemies*, Lippincott, 1909.

Snow, K., *Insects & Diseases*, Halsted Press, 1974.

Standen, Anthony, *Insect Invaders*, Houghton, Mifflin, 1943.

Thorp, R. W., and Woodson, W. D., *The Black Widow Spider*, Dover, 1976. (Original edition, 1945.)

U.S. Air Force, Aerospace Medical Division, *Venomous Arthropod Handbook*, U.S. Government Printing Office, 1977.

U.S. Department of Agriculture, *Be Safe From Insects in Recreation Areas*, U.S. Government Printing Office, 1972.

U.S. Department of Agriculture, *Controlling Wasps*, U.S. Government Printing Office, 1972 (Home and Garden Bulletin No. 122).

U.S. Department of Agriculture, *Insects. The Yearbook of Agriculture*, U.S. Government Printing Office, 1952. (See especially section on Livestock and Insects, pp. 657–676.)

U.S. Department of Health, Education, and Welfare, Center for Disease Control, *Envenomization*, DHEW Publication No. (HSM) 72-8121, 1970.

U.S. Department of the Navy, Naval Medical School, *Medical Entomology*, The School, 1966, 1968.

U.S. Departments of the Navy, the Army, and the Air Force, *Military Entomology Operational Handbook*, U.S. Government Printing Office, December, 1971.

Washburn, F. L., *Injurious Insects and Useful Birds*, Lippincott, 1918.

Wigglesworth, V. B., *Insect Physiology*. Methuen, 1966. (Advanced.)

Wigglesworth, V. B., *Insects and the Life on Man*, Halsted Press, 1976.

Zinsser, Hans, *Rats, Lice, and History*, Little, Brown, 1935.

# ARTICLES

Arnold, R. E., "Poison! A Catalog of Dangerous Plants and Animals" (spiders), *Sports Illustrated,* September, 1976.

Arnold, R. E., "Vespidae," *Sports Illustrated,* December, 1976.

Barnard, J. II., "Studies of 400 Hymenoptera Sting Deaths in the United States," *Journal of Allergy and Clinical Immunology,* May 1973, vol. 52, no. 5, pp. 259–264.

Brody, J. E., "Two Zoologists Find Ants Using Tools," *The New York* Times, April 4, 1976.

Brownell, G. G., "The Sting of Death," *Good Housekeeping,* August, 1976.

Cooke, J. A., and others, "Urticaria Caused by Tarantula Hairs," *American Journal of Tropical Medicine and Hygiene,* 1973, vol. 22, no. 1, pp. 130 ff.

Davis, M. C., "Horse-Faced Flies," *Insect World Digest,* November/December, 1975.

Desowitz, R. S., "The Fly That Would Be King," *Natural History,* February, 1977.

Desowitz, R. S., "How the Wise Men Brought Malaria to Africa," *Natural History,* October, 1976.

Djerassi, C., and others, "Insect Control of the Future," *Science,* April 18, 1975.

Edwards, J. S., "Insect Assasins," *Scientific American,* June, 1960.

Eisner, T., and others, "2,5–Dichlorophenol (from Ingested Herbicide?) in Defensive Secretion of Grasshopper," *Science,* April 16, 1971.

Gary, N. E., "Possible Approaches to Controlling the African Honey Bee," *American Bee Journal,* No. 11, 1971, vol. III, pp. 426–429.

Gilbert, B., "I've Got You Under My Skin" (fleas), *Sports Illustrated,* August 15, 1977.

Graham, F., Jr., "Pest Control: Parasites in Search of Friends," *Audubon Magazine,* January 1978.

Green, Timothy, "A Man's Obsession Reveals the Riches of a Hidden World," *Smithsonian,* November, 1977.

Greenberg, B., "Flies and Disease," *Scientific American,* July, 1965.

Gwynne, P., and Smith, V. E., "Fire Ants," *Newsweek,* April 26, 1976. (See also reply by A. Wolff in *Audubon Magazine,* July, 1976.)

Holden, Constance, "Mirex: Persistent Pesticide on Its Way Out," *Science,* October 15, 1976.

Humphrey, J. H., "The Challenge of Parasitic Diseases," *Bulletin of the Atomic Scientists,* March, 1977.

*Insect World Digest,* "The Man-Hating African Honeybee," *Insect World Digest,* March/April, 1973.

Lyon, W. F., "My Experience With the African Honeybee," *Gleanings in Bee Culture,* November, 1974.

McKelvey, J. J., Jr., "The Rehabilitation of the 'Killer Bee,'" *R. F. Illustrated* (Rockefeller Foundation), September, 1977.

Marx, J. L., "Applied Ecology: Showing the Way to Better Insect Control," *Science,* March 4, 1977.

National Academy of Sciences, *Pest Control: Strategies for the Future,* 1972.

Ormerod, W. E., "Ecological Effect of Control of African Trypanosomiasis" (sleeping sickness), *Science,* February 27, 1976.

Parrish, H. M., "Analysis of 460 Fatalities from Venomous Animals in the United States," *American Journal of Medical Science,* 1963, vol. 245, pp. 129–141.

Paust, Gil, "The Stabbers, Slashers and Suckers," *Field and Stream*, July, 1975.

Petrunkevitch, A., "The Spider and the Wasp," *Scientific American*, August, 1952.

Piel, G., and Schneirla, T. C., "The Army Ant," *Scientific American*, June, 1948.

Reisman, R. E., "Danger! Stinging Insects" (interview), *Reader's Digest*, July, 1976.

Rosten, Leo, "The Might of the Midgets," *Saturday Review*, April 17, 1976. (A light-hearted look at insects, unfortunately referred to as anthropods. *Anthropos* is "human" in Greek.)

*Science News*, "Insect Resistance Climbs, Academy Says," *Science News*, February 14, 1976.

Smith, H. Allen, "There's No Hotfoot Like a Scorpion Bite," *Smithsonian*, February, 1976.

Snell, David, "Fever Tick Crashes Roundup, Causes Trouble on the Range," *Smithsonian*, October, 1977.

Sterba, J. P., "Tarantulas Are Eluding Federal Regulatory Web," *The New York Times*, August 9, 1976.

Taylor, O. R., and Williamson, G. B., "Current Status of the Africanized Honey Bee in Northern South America," *American Bee Journal*, March, 1975.

*Time*, "The Bugs Are Coming!" *Time*, July 12, 1976.

Tobe, S. S., "How Tsetse Flies Reproduce," *Insect World Digest*, November/December, 1974.

Topoff, H. R., "The Social Behavior of Army Ants," *Scientific American*, November, 1972.

Topoff, Howard, "Ants on the March," *Natural History*, December, 1975.

Wolff, A., "Making Mountains Out of Fire Ant Mounds," *Audubon Magazine*, July, 1976. (Reply to article in *Newsweek* by P. Gwynn and V. E. Smith).

Wolff, Anthony, "Building a Better Bug Trap," *The New York Times Magazine*, November 28, 1976.

# Index

Acrobat ants, 59
Adrenalin, 36, 40, 41, 58
*Aedes* mosquitoes, 121, 123
Africa, 44, 60, 157
   diseases, 91, 121, 123-124, 126, 127-129
   honeybees, 11-15
African honeybees, 11-15
   and Brazilian bees, 13-14
   moving toward U.S., 14-15
"Alarm odors," 55
Alkaloids, 29
American Academy of Allergy, 74
American Indians, 47
American Medical Association, 63
American Society of Allergists, 36
Amoebic dysentery, 116
*Anopheles* mosquitoes, 121, 123, 125
*Anopheles aquasalis,* 124
Anthrax, 91

Antibodies, 118-120
Ants, 19, 27, 34, 53, 59-67, 116-117, 167
   acrobat ants, 59
   Argentine ants, 59
   bite (or sting), 20, 36, 59-61
   bodies, 59
   deaths caused by, 20, 36
   fire ants, 60-61, 63, 152, 154
   harvester ants, 60, 63-64
   tools, 165
   venom, 64-65
Aphids, 17
Appendages, 17
Arachnids, 17, 77, 102
Arana Cave, Spain, 57
Argentine ants, 59
Aristophanes, 10
Arizona
   scorpions, 68
Army ants, 60, 167
Arnold, Robert E., 42

**179**

Arthropods, 17-18, 101
  characteristics, 17
  death caused by bite or
    sting of, 20
Assassin bugs, 17, 66, 97
*Audubon Magazine,* 63
Australia
  ants, 60

Babesiosis, 132
Bacteria, 119, 120, 158
Baldfaced hornets, 48, 49, 52
Barham, R. H., 24
Beagle-Atkins, J. W., 14
Bedbugs, 17, 98
Beekeeping, 56-57
Bees, 14, 19, 25, 27-28, 34,
    38, 44, 53-59, 167
  African honeybees, 11-15
  and animals, 12-13
  bodies, 53
  deaths caused by, 14, 16,
    20, 36
  honeybees, 11-15, 28, 38,
    53, 54-56, 57
  sting, 11-13, 14-16, 20, 36,
    55-56
  as weapons, 14
Beetles, 44, 116-117, 137, 145
  blister beetles, 69-70
  bombadier beetles, 66
Bird-eating spiders, 53, 102
Bites, 27, 28
  ants, 20, 36, 59-61
  bugs, 97-99
  centipedes, 42, 99-100, 101
  flies, 87, 89, 90-92, 118, 127
  mosquitoes, 42, 95

scorpions, 20, 31
snakes, 20, 31, 36
spiders, 20, 31, 36, 42, 101,
    105, 108
ticks, 79
  *See also* Stings
Black Death, 138-140
Black flies, 88-89, 90, 127
  bite, 90
  and dogs, 90
Black widow spiders, 32-33,
    104-107
"Blind staggers," 92
Blister beetles, 69-70
Bloodsuckers, 26, 86
Blowflies, 118
Bluebottle flies, 118
Body segments (arthropods),
    17
Bombadier beetles, 66
Botflies, 92
Brazil, 44, 57
  Chagas's disease, 132
  honeybees, 13-14
Bromeliad epiphyte, 125
Brown dog ticks, 80-81
Brown recluse spiders, 107-108
Brownell, George B., 41
Brown-tail moths, 73
Buboes, 138
Bubonic plague, 116, 138
Buffalo gnats, 90
Bugs, 17, 18, 44, 84
  assassin bugs, 17, 66, 97
  bite, 97-99
  diseases caused by, 134
  bedbugs, 17, 98

kissing bugs, 97-98, 131, 158
water bugs, 97
wheel bugs, 98-99
Bumblebees, 53, 54-55, 66
nests, 53
sting, 55
Bushmen, 44
*Buthus occitanus,* 30

Cabbage maggots, 150
Cacao industry, 125
California
farmers, 57
Cantharidin, 69
Caribbean
tarantulas, 103
Carpenter ants, 59
Caterpillars, 43, 71-73, 83, 116-117
effect of venom, 72-73
size, 72
Cattle, 93, 128-130
Center for Disease Control, 79
Centipedes, 17, 99-101
bite, 42, 99-100, 101
size, 99
Central America, 16, 33, 44, 97
diseases, 121, 126
*Centruroides* (scorpions), 30, 34, 68
*gertachi,* 30
*sculpturatus,* 30
*suffusus,* 30
Chagas's disease, 97, 131-132, 166
Chalcid, 83

Chauvin, Rémy, 64-65, 66, 154
Chewing insects, 25
Chiggers, 84, 86, 160
Chigoe fleas, 28, 84
Chimpanzees, 163-164
*Chirimacha,* 166
Cholera, 116
Cicada, 17, 48
Clothing, protective, 12
Cobra, 32
Cockroaches, 117, 143
diseases caused by, 134
Colorado potato beetles, 145
Conenose bugs, 97, 98, 134
Cotton bollworms, 158
Crabill, Ralph E., Jr., 103
Cuba, 96
Culex mosquitoes, 121, 123
Cyclodiene, 150
Cyrene, 143

DDT, 145-151
Dams, 125
Darwin, Charles, 132
*Dead Ducks,* 142
Deaths caused by
ants, 20, 36
arthropods, 20
bees, 14, 16, 20, 36
black widow spiders, 105, 107
centipedes, 100
flies, 115-116
hornets, 20
hymenoptera, 20, 36
insecticides, 147-148
scorpions, 16, 20, 67

Deaths caused by (*continued*)
  snakes, 20, 36
  spiders, 16, 20, 36, 105, 107
  wasps, 20, 36
  yellow jackets, 20
Deer flies, 135
Dengue, 121, 123
Department of Agriculture,
  U.S., 93-94
Desowitz, Robert, 124
"Dial-a-bug" service, 162-163
Dieldrin, 152
Diphtheria, 116
Diseases, 86, 91, 113, 115,
  116, 121, 123, 133-137,
  146
  Africa, 91, 121, 123-124,
    126, 127-129
  Chagas's disease, 97, 131-
    132, 166
  elephantiasis, 91, 123
  encephalitis, 121, 123
  filariasis, 91, 121, 123
  malaria, 21, 121, 123-127,
    146
  plague, 138-140, 146
  Rocky Mountain spotted
    fever, 79
  sleeping sickness, 127-130
  South America, 97, 121,
    126, 131-132
  typhoid, 116, 146
  typhus, 86, 115
  vectors of, 21, 133-137
  yellow fever, 96, 121, 123,
    146
Diseases caused by
  beetles, 137
  bugs, 134
  cockroaches, 134
  fleas, 86, 133, 135
  flies, 91-95, 115-118, 127,
    134, 135, 137
  gnats, 135, 137
  kissing bugs, 131
  lice, 136
  millipedes, 133
  mites, 133
  mosquitoes, 95-97, 121-125,
    136
  moths, 137
  ticks, 133
Dog flies, 28, 89
Dragonfly, 150
Driver ants, 60
Dysentery, 116

East Indian horsefly, 25, 27
Elephantiasis, 91, 123
Emergency first aid. *See* First
  aid
Encephalitis, 121, 123
England
  Black Death, 139
Entomologist, 17
Environmental Protection
  Agency, 97, 158
Epidemic, 118
Epinephrine, 40
*Erebus agrippina*, 44
*Euglossa cordata*, 25
Exoskeleton, 17
Eye gnats, 135
"Eye worms," 91

*Field & Stream*, 42

Filariasis, 91, 121, 123
Fire ants, 60-61, 63, 152, 154
  nests, 61
  sting, 63
First aid, 31-32, 110
  bee stings, 56
  caterpillar venom, 73
  centipede bites, 101
  fire ant stings, 63
  scorpion stings, 69
Flanders, Michael, 142
Flannel moths, 73
Fleas, 82, 84-87, 138, 139,
  146, 160, 165
  bloodsuckers, 86
  chigoe fleas, 28, 84
  diseases caused by, 86, 133,
  135
  and dogs & cats, 85-86
  mouth parts, 86
  size, 84
  trained, 86
Flies, 44, 52, 82, 87-95, 118,
  146, 148, 151, 160
  bite, 87, 89, 90-92, 118, 127
  black flies, 88-89, 99, 127,
  134
  botflies, 92
  deaths caused by, 115-116
  diseases caused by, 91-95,
  115-118, 127, 134, 135
  dog flies, 28, 89
  greenhead, 89
  horn flies, 161
  horse flies, 25, 27, 82-83,
  87-88
  no-see-ums, 87, 92

  screwworm flies, 92-95, 160-
  161
  tsetse flies, 127, 130, 137,
  157
  wings, 87
Fluke, 81-82
Formic acid, 60, 64, 65, 66
*Formica rufa,* 66
*Formicinae,* 60, 64
France, Vosges Mountains, 65
Frogs, 30, 33
Funnel web spiders, 32-33

Gangrene, 116
Gnats, 90, 135, 137, 160
Gonorrhea, 116
*Good Housekeeping,* 41
Grasshoppers, 150
Greeks, ancient, 14
Greenhead (fly), 89
Gulf Coast ticks, 93
Guyana, 124

Havana, Cuba, 96
Harvester ants, 60, 63-64
  nests, 64
  sting, 63
Hemiptera, 17, 97
Herzog, Arthur, 16
Hippopotamus botflies, 92
Hocking, Brian, 90
Honey, 13
Honeybees, 28, 53, 54-56, 57
  African, 11-15
  North American, 57
  serum, 13
  shortage, 57
  sting, 55-56

Honeybees (*continued*)
  Stone Age, 57
  venom, 38
Horn flies, 161
Hornets, 11, 34, 38, 52, 53
  baldfaced hornets, 48, 49, 52
  deaths caused by, 20
  nests, 49
  sting, 20, 29
Horse flies, 25, 27, 82-83, 87-88
  size, 87
Hubbell, Y., 14
Hymenoptera, 34, 53
  deaths caused by, 20
  sting, 20, 36

Ichneumon (wasp)
  and caterpillars, 83
Immunization, 37-41, 120
India, 124
  bees, 14
Indians, 47, 67
Insect Sting Kit, 40
Insecta, 17, 18
Insecticides, 121, 145-156
  birth deaths from, 147
  human deaths from, 147-148
  immunity to, 148, 152
  mutations caused from, 150
  spraying, 154-155
Insects Affecting Man Research Laboratory, 158
*Insects Injurious to the Household,* 113

International Center of Insect Physiology, 157
Ic moth caterpillars, 73
Ireland
  Black Death, 139

Jicarilla Apache Indians, 47
Jigger fleas, 84

*Karakurt,* 104
Kennedy, Donald, 152
Kepone, 154
"Killer bees," 14-15, 44
Kissing bugs, 97-98, 131, 158

Ladybugs, 158
Lake Erie, 52
*Latrodectus m. mactans,* 32-33, 107
Leishmaniasis, 132
Leprosy, 116
Libya, 143
Lice, 82, 113, 136, 146
Loa loa, 91
Locusts, 143
Los Angeles County, 109
*Loxosceles lactae,* 109
*Loxosceles reclusa,* 107
*Lycosa erythrognatha,* 32-33
Lyon, William F., 12-13

Maggots, 92, 94-95, 150
Malaria, 21, 121, 123-127, 146
Marquis, Don, 76
Mayas, 67
Medic Alert, 40
*Megasoma elephas,* 44
Methoprene, 161

Mexican bedbugs, 98
Mexico, 151
  scorpions, 16
  tarantulas, 103
Mice, 33
Michigan, 162
Microorganisms, 117, 119-120, 158
*Military Entomology Operational Handbook*, 36
Millipedes, 101, 133'
Mirex, 154-155
Mites, 82, 83-84, 113
  disease caused by, 133
Morocco, 124
Mosquito repellers, 96-97, 160
Mosquitoes, 27, 82-83, 146
  bite, 42, 95
  breeding areas, 124-125
  diseases caused by, 95-97, 121-125, 136
Moths, 44, 73, 137
Mouth parts (insects), 26-27
Mud daubers, 48, 51
Mutillid wasps, 52
Myriapods, 17
*Myrmicea*, 64
*Myrmecia gulosa*, 59-60

Nantucket Island, 132
Napoleon, 115
Nash, Ogden, 46
National Academy of Sciences, 151, 156
National Career Institute, 154
*Natural History*, 124
Nelco Laboratories, 40, 59
Nematodes, 121

Nests, 49-51, 163
  bumblebees, 53
  fire ants, 61
  harvester ants, 64
  hornets, 49
  mud daubers, 51
  *polistes*, 49
  wasps, 49-51
  yellow jackets, 49
Nettling hairs, 43, 71
Neurotoxic venom, 29-30
New Jersey
  beekeeping, 56-57
  encephalitis, 123
New Jersey Agricultural Experiment Station, 96
Newman, L. H., 21
*Newsweek*, 63
Nicotine, 144
No-see-ums, 87, 92

Organophosphates, 147-148
Ormerod, W. E., 130
Overgrazing, 130

*Pangonia longirostris*, 25, 27
Parasites, 81-83, 158
Parathion, 148
Paris green, 145
Parrish, H. M., 20
Pathogens, 119, 120
Peloponnesian War, 139
Pennsylvania State University, 38
Peru, 166
Pfadt, R. E., 165-166
Pheromones, 55, 157
Phlebotomus fever, 91

Phoenicians, 14
*Phoneutria nigriventer*, 32, 33
Plague, 138-140, 146
Poisons. *See* Venom
Poliomyelitis, 116
*Polistes*, 48, 49
Pollen, 19, 54
Pollination, 57
Potato beetles, 145
Praying mantis, 19, 158
Protective clothing, 12
Protozoans, 119
Public Health Service, U.S., 140
*Pulex irritans*, 86
Pyrethrum, 144

Rain forests, 124-125
Rattlesnakes, 32, 33-34
Rats, 138, 139
*Rats, Lice, and History*, 113
Red bugs, 84
Reed, Walter, 96
Reisman, Robert E., 74
Repellents (mosquito), 96-97, 160
Rhinoceros beetles, 44
*Rhinocricus*, 101
Rice fields, 124
River blindness, 126-127
Rocky Mountain spotted fever, 79
Rotenone, 144, 146

Saddleback caterpillars, 72
*Salmonella* bacteria, 120
Sand flies, 90, 132, 137
Sawflies, 27

Scale insects, 17
Scarlet fever, 116
*Science*, 130
Scorpions, 17, 31, 33, 34, 67-69, 143, 160
  deaths caused by, 16, 20, 67
  early names, 69
  size, 67-68
  sting, 20, 29-30, 42, 67, 69
Scotland
  Black Death, 139
Screwworm flies, 92-95, 160-161
*Scutigera forceps*, 99
Sea snakes, 33
Sea wasp jellyfish, 33
Sensors, 17
Shield bugs, 17
Sleeping sickness, 127-130
Snakes, 30
  bite, 20, 31, 36
  deaths caused by, 20, 36
  rattlesnakes, 32, 33-34
Social insects, 51, 163
*Solenopsis*, 152
South America, 16, 33, 44, 60, 166, 167
  bird-eating spiders, 102
  diseases, 97, 121, 126, 131-132
  Indians, 67
  tarantulas, 103
Spain
  Arana Cave, 57
Spiders, 17, 26, 31-33, 53, 101-110, 160
  bite, 20, 31, 36, 42, 101, 105, 108

black widow, 32-33, 104-107
bodies, 102
brown recluse, 107-108
deaths caused by, 16, 20, 36, 105, 107
and wasps, 52-53
Spraying poison, 64-66
ants, 60
assassin bugs, 66
bombadier beetles, 66
bumblebees, 66
Squirting apparatus, 43
Stable flies, 28, 89
Sterilization, 160-161
"Sting of Death, The," 41
Stings, 27-28, 34-36, 110
allergic reactions, 34-36
ants, 20, 36, 59-61
avoiding, 58-59
bees, 11-13, 14-16, 20, 36, 55-56
fire ants, 63
harvester ants, 63
hornets, 20, 29
hymenoptera, 20, 36
scorpions, 20, 29-30, 42, 67, 69
wasps, 20, 29, 36, 42, 52
yellow jackets, 20, 41
*See also* Bites
Stink bugs, 44
Stone Age, 57
*Swarm, The,* 16
Syria, 124

Tanzania, 124
Tapeworms, 81-82

Tarantulas, 32-33, 102-104
as pets, 102-104
and wasps, 53
Taylor, Orley R., 14-15
Termites, 25, 148
Ticks, 77-81, 93, 132, 138, 157, 160
disease caused by, 133
and dogs, 80
removing, 79
size, 79
Toads, 30
Tobacco budworms, 158
Toxins, 29
*Trechona venosa,* 32-33
Tree bees, 14
Trichina, 81-82
Trinidad, 125
Tropical tarantulas, 32-33
Trypanosomiasis, 127, 131-132
Tsetse flies, 127, 130, 137, 157
Tuberculosis, 116
Tularemia, 86
Tussock moths, 73
Typhoid, 116, 146
Typhus, 86, 115

*Urtica,* 71
Urticating hairs, 43, 71

Vectors of disease, 21, 133-137
Velvet ants, 52
Venezuela, 124, 167
Venom, 29-34
ants, 64-65
caterpillars, 72-73

Venom (*continued*)
  collecting for immunization,
    39, 40
  on contact, 71
  effect of, 29, 30
  honeybees, 38
  millepedes, 101
  potency, 32-33
  stored, 30
Vesicating arthropods, 69
Viet Nam, 125
Viruses, 119, 158
Vosges Mountains, France, 65

WBE, 37-40
Washburn, F. L., 94
Wasps, 19, 27-28, 34, 38, 48-
    54, 158-159, 160
  bodies, 48
  deaths caused by, 20, 36
  nests, 49-51
  social, 51
  and spiders, 52-53

sting, 20, 29, 36, 42, 52
  and tarantulas, 53
Water bugs, 97
Water fleas, 133
Webs (spider), 107
Wheel bugs, 98-99
Whole body extract, 37-40
Wild bees, 57
Wolf spiders, 32-33
Wolff, Anthony, 63
World Health Organization,
    21, 121
Worms, 81-82

Yellow fever, 96, 121, 123,
    146
Yellow flea beetles, 44
Yellow jackets, 34, 38, 47-48
  deaths caused by, 20
  nests, 49
  sting, 20, 41

Zinsser, Hans, 113
Zootoxin, 29

# Picture Credits

Page

15  U. S. Department of Agriculture

18  From *Le Monde des Fourmis* by Rémy Chauvin, Librarie Plon

19  Military Entomology Operational Handbook

26  D. E. Billman, "Arachnidism, with Report of a Case," Nav. Med. Bull., 47(6) : 975-982 (1947)

39  Top: Heckman, Department of Entomology, Pennsylvania State University

Bottom: Harlan Berger, Pennsylvania State University

43  Department of Health, Education and Welfare

48  U. S. Department of Agriculture

49  U. S. Department of Agriculture

50  Top: U. S. Department of Agriculture

Bottom: Harlan Berger, Pennsylvania State University

51  Courtesy of Terry L. Biery, U.S.A.F. School of Aerospace Medicine

54  U. S. Department of Agriculture

60  Scientific American

61  U. S. Department of Agriculture

62  U. S. Department of Agriculture

65  From *Le Monde des Fourmis* by Rémy Chauvin, Librarie Plon

Page

68 Hugh L. Keegan, Ph.D., University of Mississippi Medical Center

70 U. S. Department of Agriculture

71 *Pest Control*

72 U. S. Department of Agriculture

78 From *Destructive and Useful Insects* by C. L. Metcalf, W. P. Flint, and R. L. Metcalf. Copyright 1951 by the McGraw Hill Book Company. Reprinted by permission.

80 Dr. Roger W. Williams, School of Public Health, Columbia University

81 *Military Entomology Operational Handbook*

82 From A. S. Pearse, *Introduction to Parasitology*, 1942. Courtesy of Charles C. Thomas, Publisher.

83 Dr. Roger W. Williams, School of Public Health, Columbia University

85 *Military Entomology Operational Handbook*

88 From *Destructive and Useful Insects* by C. L. Metcalf, W. P. Flint, and R. L. Metcalf. Copyright 1951 by the McGraw Hill Book Company. Reprinted by permission.

89 *Military Entomology Operational Handbook*

91 U. S. Department of Agriculture

93 U. S. Department of Agriculture

94 U. S. Department of Agriculture

98 U. S. Department of Agriculture

100 Hugh L. Keegan, Ph.D., University of Mississippi Medical Center

103 U. S. Department of Agriculture

106 D. E. Billman, "Arachnidism, with Report of a Case," Nav. Med. Bull. 47(6) : 975-982 (1947)

109 U. S. Department of Agriculture

PICTURE CREDITS

Page

114  Top: From Riley and Johannsen, *Handbook of Medical Entomology*, Comstock Publishing Company.
Bottom: *Military Entomology Operational Handbook*

115  From *Destructive and Useful Insects* by C. L. Metcalf, W. P. Flint, and R. L. Metcalf. Copyright 1951 by the McGraw Hill Book Company. Reprinted by permission.

116  U. S. Department of Agriculture

122  U. S. Department of Agriculture

126  Dr. Roger W. Williams, School of Public Health, Columbia University

128  Marion Kaplan

129  Rockefeller Foundation

131  Dr. Roger W. Williams, School of Public Health, Columbia University

149  Vernon J. Tipton, Ph.D., Center for Health and Environmental Studies, Brigham Young University

153  U. S. Department of Agriculture

155  U. S. Department of Agriculture

159  U. S. Department of Agriculture

164  American Museum of Natural History

168  U. S. Department of Agriculture